"Someone to Tell It To *represents one of the most compassionate outreaches by the Church to those who are troubled by groanings that cannot be uttered. The prayerful listening and counseling that these two men do is one of the most effective instruments for the healing of minds and souls that I know about anywhere in the world. What a treasure it is for us to have these men serving so faithfully at work that is essential and, yet, has been left largely undone."*—Tony Campolo, PhD. Eastern University Sociology Department

"*Relationships, the kind that connect people in ways only the Gospel makes possible. That's what* Someone To Tell It To *is all about. And that's why their vision has my support.*"—Dr. Larry Crabb. Author, Psychologist

"*Too often we suffer alone, afraid to share the truth of our insides, afraid to be authentic with others, particularly when we are suffering. That greatly exacerbates pain and prolongs it. A big part of my message, when discussing my friendship with Mister Rogers, is to encourage people to come out of their hiding. Cop to their pain. There are people out there who will listen with healing presence and compassion, and I have just discovered two more. They are Michael Gingerich and Thomas Kaden, who have recently embarked on a mission they have named, brilliantly enough,* Someone To Tell It To. *I learned of their hopes to help coax people out of their isolation, as Fred coaxed me out of mine. I believe one of the greatest struggles of humankind is individual isolation, particularly with suffering. With great personal courage themselves, these two guys are committed to tackling that struggle head on. I endorse them without reservation, and admire them both greatly. I am proud to call them my brothers, my friends.*"—Tim Madigan, Arlington, TX
Author of I'm Proud of You: My Friendship with Fred Rogers

Someone To Tell It To:
SHARING LIFE'S JOURNEY

Michael Gingerich & Tom Kaden

WESTBOW°
PRESS
A DIVISION OF THOMAS NELSON
& ZONDERVAN

Scripture quotations from The Message
Copyright © by Eugene H. Peterson 1993, 1994, 1995, 1996, 2000, 2001, 2002. Used by permission of NavPress Publishing Group.

New Revised Standard Version Bible, copyright © 1989, Division of Christian Education of the National Council of the Churches of Christ in the United States of America. Used by permission. All rights reserved.

Scripture taken from the New King James Version. Copyright © 1979, 1980, 1982 by Thomas Nelson, inc. Used by permission. All rights reserved.

WestBow Press books may be ordered through booksellers or by contacting:

WestBow Press
A Division of Thomas Nelson & Zondervan
1663 Liberty Drive
Bloomington, IN 47403
www.westbowpress.com
1 (866) 928-1240

ISBN: 978-1-4908-3903-5 (sc)
ISBN: 978-1-4908-3904-2 (hc)
ISBN: 978-1-4908-3902-8 (e)

Library of Congress Control Number: 2014910890

Printed in the United States of America.

WestBow Press rev. date: 06/24/2014

For Kathy and Sarah, Adam, David and Matthew, Lillian, Luke, Madelyn and Mya, Kate and Janelle, Lilyanna, Emma, and Emmett . You are our inspiration. You are our life. You are our joy.

What really knocks me out is a book that, when you're all done reading it, you wish the author that wrote it was a terrific friend of yours and you could call him up on the phone whenever you felt like it. That doesn't happen much, though.

—J.D. Salinger

Authors' Note

God can do anything, you know—far more than you
could ever imagine or guess or request in your wildest
dreams! He does it not by pushing us around but by
working within us, his Spirit deeply and gently within us.

—Ephesians 3:20, *The Message*

$524.84

We value every donation to the mission of Someone To Tell It To as
a treasured gift. We try our best to express gratitude for every $10
commitment, as well as the $5,000 yearly pledge. Each gift helps us to fulfill
the calling that God has placed upon our lives. We live in awe of God's
abundant faithfulness. But there was one donation this year, especially,
that caused us to pause, give thanks, and simply rest in wonder …

It was the last day of the month, and it was time to pay our local, state,
and federal taxes, thousands of dollars. What we owed depleted our bank
account to almost nothing. Yet there was still one bill that we needed to
pay—the down payment for this book. $524.84. The bill was due the
following day, and we didn't know where we would get the money to pay
it. We were certain that we were going to miss the deadline for publishing
this book.

But that evening, one of us had dinner with two of our closest friends. As they were leaving, totally unaware of our financial situation and the acute anxiety we were feeling about it, they left a check to support Someone To Tell It To's mission—*for $525!* Enough to pay the bill and with a little extra leftover.

This was when we knew this project of sharing life's journey was meant to be.

We hope that by reading these stories something may be evoked or stirred in you to open up your heart and share your stories too.

Acknowledgments

We are deeply indebted to the many gifts we have received this year to help make this project possible, particularly to our friends who helped to edit the book, offering their expertise, affirmation, and service—Lindsay de Bien and Kristin Sidorov.

We give special, profound thanks to Michele Eby, who worked tirelessly to make certain that our words made sense and that our message was clear. You have been a godsend to us. You helped us to find and share our voice.

To everyone who encouraged us and who wants our mission to succeed, we are blessed beyond measure. To you, we are continually grateful.

And to everyone who gave us permission to tell your story—to you who became vulnerable with us and allowed us to share intimate parts of your lives—we are deeply grateful for the inspiration that your stories offer to a broken world that is searching for healing.

Introduction

Someone to tell it to is one of the fundamental needs of human beings.

—Miles Franklin

. . . .

We can't pinpoint one specific moment when this book, and this journey together, began. There were many moments actually—many conversations, many walks, and many beers—which in essence jump-started this book and this mission about which we write. It was on one of our walks, in a community park in New Cumberland, Pennsylvania, where it all began. We go back to that park often, especially when we need to talk, reflect, pray, process, or plan. It is a sacred place for us, a place where our sacred mission had its birth.

Australian author Miles Franklin understood something profound: We are all created to share, to connect with others, emotionally, physically, and spiritually. We all want and need to be heard, to know that others listen and care. We crave intimacy. We are in a constant search for validation and for our voices to find resonance with the lives of others.

Her statement has intrigued us since the very first time we each read it. We have seen this need again and again during our years as pastors, while visiting people who have been homebound or in hospital rooms, while sitting with someone grieving the death of a loved one, or while comforting those in distress, pain, loneliness, or uncertainty. We have also experienced this need firsthand as we have grappled with our own families' challenges with cancer, financial pressures, career directions, and disability. We have learned how all of us at times vitally need to be heard. We need someone to listen so our struggles and questions become shared and not ours alone to bear.

Loneliness is part of the human condition that confronts and challenges each of us.

Don't we all need connections with others? Isn't life about the relationships we create, the people we invite into our lives, and those who invite us into theirs? Yet most of our relationships have no significant depth, no intimacy. We are carried through life, and while we connect with others in countless ways, most of those ways are superficial. We barely pierce the surface of our being; we rarely reveal the real issues in our lives.

This is why the nonprofit we started, Someone To Tell It To, is so significant. It is a safe place for all of us to express our feelings, with the assurance that we can confidently give voice to all that is on our minds, in our hearts, and on our souls. It is a place where we will not be judged or condemned. Rather, it is a place where we will be given the freedom to share our burdens so we may begin to find relief from them. It is a place where we will be given the encouragement to seek light instead of darkness, forgiveness instead of bitterness, and affirmation instead of criticism and negativity. It is a place where we can find comfort, a means to joy, and a path toward healing and abiding peace.

We believe that everyone needs someone to tell it to and that everyone needs grace and a safe place to share. We believe that everyone has a story to tell and a need to be listened to, that everyone is worthy and has something to offer, that everyone hungers for authenticity, that everyone has a need to be who they were created to be, and that everyone is meant to live an abundant life.

These beliefs are the foundation of the book *Someone To Tell It To*. When you read this book, we hope you will be encouraged to give voice to your struggles and pain, to embrace your strengths, to confront your fears, and then to be inspired to find new life again—as the people on these pages have done.

We have been preparing for this book for several years and have spent extensive time in reflection, study, prayer, discussion, and planning to create an outreach to both those of established faith and to those who are exploring what spirituality and faith could mean to them on their lives' journeys. Out of professional and personal life experiences, as well as our educational backgrounds (Tom is a graduate of Asbury Theological Seminary and Michael is a graduate of Lancaster Theological Seminary), we are answering the call to write *Someone To Tell It To: Sharing Life's Journey* so that others may find a life of hope, joy, love, and peace.

I've Never Shared This with Anyone Else Before

I don't know of anything that will help us find emotional health faster than being vulnerable with safe people.

—Donald Miller

. . . .

We can feel the pressures roll off their shoulders and melt from their hearts anytime people say to us, *"I've never shared this with anyone else before."*

It's in those moments that long-hidden secrets are revealed and long-held feelings are set free.

We see the sense of freedom they feel when they say that. It's a sense of relief that a burden they've been carrying has been lifted, especially when their burden is shared in safety and in trust. It's when light is shed on a corner of darkness within them that healing can begin.

We're certainly not suggesting that people should expose every experience or thought or fear to everyone they meet. If you see what's often revealed on the walls of Facebook or through the tweets on Twitter, you may agree that, sometimes, people publicly expose too much. But we do believe that it is critical to one's emotional, mental, spiritual, and physical well-being to have safe people with whom to share. We all need someone with whom

1

we can open up the depths of our souls, someone with whom we can be vulnerable.

For both of us our first published essays were stories about our own vulnerability.

Michael: My essay "Fear" shared how frightened I was that my wife's cancer would return, leaving me to care for our son and his severe disabilities alone. The story detailed one way in which I reacted, all too humanly, to the prospect of great loss and great responsibility that overwhelmed me.

Tom: My essay "Uncovered" shared how I despaired at not having a job and living in my sister-in-law's attic with my wife and two young children. In my story, I revealed how unworthy I felt during that time and how I felt I was not measuring up as a husband and father to those I deeply loved.

We wrote those stories to help others, especially men, who were also living with fear and feelings of unworthiness, so they could know that they were not alone. We wrote to share how we ultimately overcame our feelings of anxiety and absence of self-esteem.

But we never could have written what would eventually become very public stories without first sharing them with our wives and with each other. Sharing with people we trusted allowed us to express the vulnerable places in our hearts. Without judgment. Without criticism. Without rejection. Without worry that we would be loved any less for it.

We all need a safe place. As Donald Miller writes, we all need safe people who allow us to be fully human, fully open, and fully who we are. There is nothing healthier than being able to open our souls to those safe people in our lives. They can begin to help free us from the burdens that weigh us down and the pain that chips away our peace and our joy.

A Safe Place

When we honestly ask ourselves which persons in our lives mean the most to us, we often find that it is those who, instead of giving advice, solutions, or cures, have chosen rather to share our pain and touch our wounds with a warm and tender hand. The friend who can be silent with us in a moment of despair or confusion, who can stay with us in an hour of grief and bereavement, who can tolerate not knowing, not curing, not healing and face with us the reality of our powerlessness, that is a friend who cares.

—Henri Nouwen

. . . .

We remember the night clearly. It's easy to recall the details of such a significant, defining moment. Here we were, both of us without jobs. Michael's had just ended that day. Tom's a few months before. Neither of us knew what we were going to do.

"Well, at least we'll be able to spend more time together," one of us said.

Neither of us knew how prophetic those words would be.

During the next few hours, we ate fish and chips, drank two Irish stouts, and as we had so many times before, shared openly and honestly about how we felt about our circumstances. We had no idea where this conversation would ultimately lead.

It was a dark season for both of us.

We committed to take advantage of this involuntary free time. We made a covenant. The first part of that covenant was that we would not hide anything from one another. We also agreed to remind one another that this was only a season; it would not last forever. We would find ways to enjoy the time we had; we would try to have some fun. We would help each other to discern where we would go next; we'd remind each other that there would be a next. We would really be present for one another. We knew there would be days of stress and anxiety and moments of confusion and uncertainty. We also knew our friendship would go on.

Early the next morning we met at a long walking path in a favorite park. We traveled it a dozen times that day. It was partially ringed by a beautiful, flowing creek, a soothing sight to walk beside. As we strode around and around the path, we admitted to each other that we were scared. Scared that our lives wouldn't be significant. Scared that financially we couldn't make it. Scared that we couldn't find jobs that would be enjoyable and fulfilling.

Week after week, we met at that park. We walked, talked, and prayed. In the meantime, we also looked for jobs. We crafted résumés. We sent letters. We scheduled interviews. Neither of us received a job offer. Weeks and months passed. Still, nothing was offered. And nothing felt right.

One day at the park, we were sitting at a picnic table eating lunch. Fearful and frustrated, one of us said, "I just don't know what to do."

It was a very vulnerable moment. And it opened a door.

"Neither do I."

We both felt intense relief. It felt good to say it aloud and share the terror and pain. It felt good knowing that we both understood. A weight was lifted.

At that moment something changed.

4

Our walk that afternoon took on a decidedly different tone. There was something more hopeful in the air. And it was then that one of us said, "What would it look like if we worked together?"

It was another vulnerable moment. What if the answer was "No way"?

Over the course of the next several weeks we started to contemplate what working together might mean. We were friends, and we had an incredible amount in common. All those weeks and months of walking and talking at the park moved our sharing from open and honest to more vulnerable. We learned more and more about ourselves—our passions, our gifts, our dreams, our calling—and one another. Ultimately, we learned we could implicitly and utterly depend on each other, that we could be truly open and vulnerable with each other, and that, as a result, working together would be a joy.

An idea emerged—a plan, a mission.

We would establish a nonprofit together. We would create the same kind of safe place for others that we had created for ourselves. We had both been doing this already, throughout our lives. We listened to others' stories, entered into their minds and hearts and lives, and provided opportunities for them to share their brokenness, burdens, joys, and hopes. We cherished those moments of emotional and spiritual intimacy in which we could help others. As Henri Nouwen describes, we yearned to be the kind of person and friend who "instead of offering advice or solutions, chooses instead to share in the darkness and pain." We both desired to make the journey with them.

It was exactly what we did for each other. And we decided we could do it with many others.

Our nonprofit, Someone to Tell It To, is who we are and who we want to be. We know what the need to unburden ourselves and express our vulnerability with someone who will not judge feels like. We know the freedom it brings and want others to know it too.

Every day we hear stories from people living with cancer; stories about what it's like to live with addictions; stories of loss and fear; stories of shame; stories about the struggle to find meaning; stories of those wrestling with their faith; stories of loneliness, rejection, and fear; stories of emptiness and longing for purpose; and stories of those who want to belong but don't know how.

We understand that telling our stories to one another and providing a safe place is necessary in our world, which often feels disconnected and individualistic, a world in which we wear masks to hide and disguise our true selves. When we take off our masks, let others in, and share our stories, we help one another.

Someday He'll Have a Conversation

Social media has given us this idea that we should all have
a posse of friends when in reality, if we have one or two
really good friends, we are lucky.

—Brené Brown

. . . .

It's a Sunday afternoon at a theme park. Thousands of people have
come through the entrance gates. Families have paid a lot of money to
be there. The neon lights on the rides flash rhythmically. Screams of fear
mixed with delight fill the air as the roller coasters take their first plunges
down steep hills. Festive music plays from the loudspeakers. Children
squeal in excitement. The inviting scent of roasting peanuts and caramel
popcorn tempts the senses.

And scores of people are talking on their cell phones.

They aren't talking with the friends or family members with whom they are
actually visiting the park; they are interacting with others instead. Whole
groups of people walking together have most members of the group on
their individual phones. Few of them are talking with each other. They
get on rides and continue talking, disconnected, with someone else. Their
minds are everywhere else but where they actually are today.

Sitting at a table having lunch is a family of three—a mother, father, and their daughter. Each of them is holding a cell phone, talking on it as they eat their lunch. The mother is checking in with her office and looking distressed. The father is calling to make an appointment to get his car serviced. The daughter is talking with her husband, who is back home at work. None of them are interacting together. They are on vacation, but they are not connecting.

An April 21, 2012, article in *The New York Times,* "The Flight from Conversation," by Sherry Turkle, examines the role that technology and all the little devices we carry around and use to communicate with others are playing in changing the way we interact, relate, and connect (or not) to one another. The article states,

> Human relationships are rich; they're messy and demanding. We have learned the habit of cleaning them up with technology … But it's a process in which we shortchange ourselves. Worse, it seems that over time we stop caring, we forget that there is a difference …
>
> We've become accustomed to a new way of being "alone together."

The article conveys a common modern dilemma. It describes a sixteen-year-old boy who uses texting as a primary form of communication and states "wistfully" that someday he'd like to learn how to have a conversation.

Someday … he'd like to learn to have a conversation.

The fact is that most of us appreciate technology. We value the things it can do for us, the ease and speed with which we can communicate, the ready information we can gain from it. And we also value communication and connection on a face-to-face, personal, and deeper level. It's virtually impossible to have a real conversation, one in which we can see into another's eyes, view another's body language, or feel another's presence via an email, through a text, on Facebook, or even over the phone. We need conversations with one another in the presence of one another to really, truly gauge one another's heart and soul. It's as simple as that.

But too often we sacrifice that kind of conversation—that deeper connection—for speed and efficiency.

It also serves well for keeping others away. The article goes on to talk about how technology is a way to keep people at a distance, "at bay ." We use it to manage others, to control them. If we keep them at a happy medium, then we're the ones who have the upper hand. If they get too close, then they know us, and many of us fear being known. But if they're too far away, then we have no connections at all. Yet we want connections because we need them; otherwise we're lonely.

With every new advance in technology—the radio, television, the computer, the smartphone—we gain something of great value. But we lose something of greater value too. We lose more and more of the ability to connect on a human, more personal level. We erode the deeper connections we need.

In a world in which we are hyperconnected technologically, we are increasingly minimally connected interpersonally. We allow the very real relationships we need to sustain our spirits and nurture our souls to slip away.

We must remember to balance our great technological innovations with our greater need for connections of substance and significance.

Both of us (Michael and Tom) work very hard to create an environment of intimacy and deep connections with our families, our friends, and one another. We are also very intentional about family mealtimes and taking days off to restore and renew. We are deliberate about spending time with our families away from other distractions. We realize how vital it is to foster and maintain relationships of meaning and significance. Mere texts, Facebook posts, and quick emails alone simply do not foster that kind of intimacy or empathy. Nurturing deeper relationships requires us to create space for people free of time constraints; to be good listeners; to ask deep, thought-provoking questions; and to make our relationships a priority.

We do our very best, even if it's imperfect, to model this with our wives, our children, and with each other as we continue to advocate for people to create more meaningful relationships.

It takes effort, time, and intention. But all of that is worth it in the infinite ways that are lives are enhanced and enriched.

Uncovered (Tom)

While we try to teach our children all about life, our children teach us what life is all about.

—Angela Schwindt

. . . .

I consider myself to be a fairly positive person now. I wasn't always that way. Living in the attic of your sister-in-law's home in the middle of the summer without air-conditioning and only a twin-sized mattress for a family of four can bring out the worst in you.

I remember the night very specifically. It was July 12. The clock read 2:00 a.m. and the temperature gauge 105. The sweat was pouring down my forehead—not only because it was hotter than a sauna in the attic, but also because I felt dejected. Earlier in the day I had received news that I didn't get the job. For the third time, I had been one of the final two candidates, and I had again been the one who lost out in the end.

Friends and family kept telling me that they "understood" because they had "been there." Did they really understand, and had they really been there? Had they really had the carpet suddenly pulled out from under them? Everything that is comfortable: job, health, house, car, freedom, future security—*gone!*

Despite the heat, I pulled the covers over my head and curled up in a little ball. The tears started streaming down my face, dampening my already sweat-dampened pillow. I felt so alone, even though I was sharing a twin-sized mattress with my wife, three-year-old daughter, and one-year-old son. I started punching my pillow and obsessing over what I was going to do.

I can't remember how long I lay in that position trying to hide my tears from my family, but it felt like an eternity. I stayed there as long as possible because it was the only place that felt safe and secure from the world around me. Those were the darkest moments of my life. As a man I can't think of anything worse than feeling as if you aren't measuring up, that you can't even take care of yourself, much less your family!

I grabbed another pillow to throw on top of my head to hide further and further from the "real world" out there. I fell asleep and awoke to a little stream of light creeping under one of the pillows. I heard a bird chirping outside the only attic window. Beneath the covers, I rolled over. I still didn't have the energy or the emotional stamina to face the world.

But then I heard laughing. My two kids were having a tickle fight on the other side of the tiny mattress. They stood up and started jumping up and down and smiling and laughing and carrying on as only kids can do. (Or can adults do that too?) The kids grabbed two pillows and started relentlessly clobbering me. I knew they wouldn't give up until I picked up a pillow and fought back. But I couldn't. I couldn't face another day "out there," so I pretended to sleep. Another strong blow to my lower back.

"Daddy! Daddy! Wake up!"

After a few minutes of trying hard to hide my feelings of shame, disappointment, and discouragement, my kids started pulling down the covers. They wanted to see my face. They pulled harder and harder. I pulled harder and harder. I wanted to stay in my little cocoon of safety and security. I heard more laughing. My kids thought this was one big game of tug of war. Didn't they know that Daddy was a loser? More laughing and pulling of the covers, until more light appeared. I finally gave up. My kids had won, but not just our tug of war game. They had won because they reminded me that they didn't care whether I had a job; they didn't care how much money I made; and they didn't care where we slept. They showed me how to appreciate joy in the moment. But joy was hard to find and maintain in that season.

We finally moved out of my sister-in-law's place and got an apartment. Our own space. But it wasn't really our own. Our landlord, who lived in the apartment below us, was constantly complaining about our kids making noise above him. How do you keep little children from playing or running or making noise? But I found myself trying, feeling constantly on edge that he'd come upstairs to talk to us about the noise or would bang a broomstick on his ceiling to announce that the kids were too loud again.

One day I had enough. I'd been home with the kids all day while my wife was at work. Our landlord had been banging on the ceiling a lot that day. I struggled, trying to keep them quiet. I felt as if I were walking on eggshells all day long. I desperately wanted out. I was frustrated and angry. I was at my wit's end.

When my wife came home, I immediately walked past her and out the door. She asked where I was going.

"I don't know. I just need to go."

I headed on foot to the closest bar. I like a beer sometimes but am no means a heavy drinker. But that night I was, and I didn't care. I wanted the heavy stuff. Shots of whiskey. And lots of it. I was in the midst of one of the most difficult seasons of my life, and I didn't see a way out. Maybe the whiskey could take away my fears and perceived failings. Nothing else could.

After a while, Michael showed up, as he had done so many times before, to simply be present with me. He slid onto the barstool next to me and for a while didn't say a word. He didn't need to. Then came the two words that I needed to hear at that moment.

"I'm sorry."

A few minutes later, he said the words he had uttered so many times before.

"I'm proud of you."

I needed to hear those words too. I was feeling lousy about myself and wasn't proud of anything about my life at that moment. He reminded me not to accept the lie that I believed at that moment—that I was worthless, no good.

Michael has been the one constant friend in my life, in addition to my wife, through everything. He is my someone to tell it to. He has encouraged and affirmed me in the moments when I need it most. He has reminded me of my goodness amid brokenness. He has reassured me that even when I have doubted my sense of self-worth that my life is meaningful and that I am loved.

Fear (Michael)

Fear is pain arising from the anticipation of evil.

—Aristotle

· ·

I had to get out of the house. My wife, Kathy, wasn't feeling well—again. Our son Matthew, who lives with severe developmental disabilities and autism, was acting out—again—hitting, pulling Kathy's hair, throwing anything not secured, and banging his head violently. Tempers flared. Frustration was boiling over. I needed some distance. I could tell that Kathy needed it too.

After realizing that a relaxing Saturday at home was not going to happen—again—I snapped. I gathered up Matthew and his wheelchair and rushed out the door.

"Where are you going?" asked Kathy.

"I don't know," I shot back brusquely.

"When are you coming back?"

"I don't know."

My words were cold, but at that moment, I didn't care. I hurried Matthew out the door and into our minivan and sped away.

I drove with no real plan or destination in mind. I didn't even know why I was driving. I only knew that something was bothering me. Something was making me incredibly angry. I needed to be alone to sort it out. But I knew that Kathy needed to be without Matthew for a while. He was safe to bring along for the ride. He can't speak, so I'd be free from interruptions and arguments.

Five hours later I was still driving and still trying to figure out what was wrong. Three years earlier, Kathy had been diagnosed with breast cancer and had undergone a partial mastectomy and seven weeks of radiation. She had other ailments (diabetes, high blood pressure, and high cholesterol), which compounded her problems. Subsequent tests showed no new signs of cancer, but for the rest of her life there would be invasive tests, careful watching, and anxious waiting.

Matthew was twenty. His disabilities and Kathy's cancer have profoundly affected our family and changed the course of our lives.

As I drove through town after town, I struggled to sort out my feelings as they collided with each other. I wondered if I would go back home. Of course, I had no reasonable idea what I'd do if I didn't. But at that point, thinking clearly was impossible.

A few hours later, Kathy called my cell phone. When I saw it was her, I didn't answer. I just wasn't ready. She called again. And again. Each time I let it ring. I was still too angry and confused to know what to say.

Sometime later I answered her call.

"How are you doing?" she asked hesitantly.

"I don't know."

"Where are you?"

"Driving." I still wasn't ready for conversation or disclosure.

"When are you coming back?"

"I don't know."

"Are you coming back?"

"I don't know."

A long silence followed, both of us not knowing what to say and neither of us wanting to break the connection. We remained like that, on the phone, not talking, for close to forty-five minutes. In that long silence, I turned the car toward home.

When we arrived, I brought Matthew into the house and got him settled. I still didn't know what to say to Kathy. I went straight to the walk-in closet in our bedroom and stood inside, not certain what to do next. Do I stay? Do I drive some more? I realized why I had gone to my closet. It was the only place in the entire world that was entirely mine to control.

Kathy came to the door and stood looking at me. "Can you tell me what's wrong?"

Without thinking, the words shot out. "I'm afraid."

"I know you are," she wisely replied.

It all began to become clear. "I'm afraid that you'll get sick again. I'm tired of all the tests. I'm frustrated that there's always something wrong with your health. I'm afraid that I'm going to have to raise Matthew on my own, and when I think about that, I don't know if I can do it. Sometimes, when I look ahead, it is just too much. So I'm afraid."

There it was. Fear. I had finally recognized it. I had finally recognized the source of my anger and frustration.

As Kathy and I put Matthew to bed, we spent the rest of the evening opening our hearts, sharing our most painful fears, and helping each

17

other keep the darkness at bay. When you live with a child who has such disabilities and needs constant care, there are more days and moments like that one than I'd care to admit. Days of fear. Days of frustration. Days of futility.

I didn't know who else to talk with that day. I didn't know who else would accept me as vulnerable as I was. It was a lonely, painful feeling. I didn't know where to go with my anger and fear.

I didn't know Tom then. But thank God I do now. He allows me and encourages me to share my fears, express my frustrations, and explore what seems to be futile. Then he helps me regain a more balanced perspective. I can tell him all about it, sugarcoating nothing, and he will listen. Tom is my someone to tell it to, and that changes everything. More than anyone besides Kathy and our other two sons, Tom sees and knows what it's like living my life every day—the joys and the burdens, the limitations and the blessings. I will never be able to thank him enough for that.

No One Ever Asks

One of the most valuable things we can do to heal one another is listen to each other's stories.

—Rebecca Falls

. . . .

"No one ever takes the time to ask me what I'm interested in. They have no idea about all the things I like."

It was a defining moment in our conversation. We were just meeting him for the first time. His fiancée, who was with him, we already knew. It would have been easy to write him off. He looked as if he didn't want to be there, as if he really didn't care about talking to us or about his wedding. It seemed as if he was enduring this meeting to please his fiancée and to humor us. At first sight, he was intimidating: tall and husky, like a football player. He wore a knit cap pulled down to his eyes. His face was bearded and unsmiling. It took some time to engage him in the conversation. But then a song came on in the background at the restaurant where we were meeting. He quietly began to sing along. We were surprised that he even knew it. It was a song from the '80s. He was twenty-six. It was on the charts well before his time.

His fiancée looked at us and said, "It's his ADD."

Her comment brought him back to our conversation.

"Yeah. I've had it since I was a kid in school. It was always getting me in trouble. I hear music, and then I am drawn to it."

One of us asked, "What kind of music do you like?"

"Everything," he replied, engaged. "Classical. Maybe we outta have 'Moonlight Sonata' at the wedding. Rock. Pop. Billy Joel. Elton John. I love Sinatra, the whole Rat Pack. Musicals."

"Musicals? Wow. Which ones do you like?"

"*Lion King. Cats. Les Miz. Phantom.*"

We never would have guessed it. He looked like one of the least likely guys to love that kind of music. He quickly began opening up more about his life, the wedding, their relationship, and how they initially bonded over music. He was enthusiastic and talkative.

That's when he quietly exclaimed, "No one ever takes the time to ask me what I'm interested in. They have no idea about all the things I like. No one ever listens to me."

No one ever takes the time. No one ever asks. No one ever has any idea. No one ever listens. Here was this big, initially sullen-looking guy, his eyes wide now, animated, smiling, sharing some really basic things about himself and who he is that he was rarely ever invited to share. How often do we write others off simply because of their appearance or their initial demeanor? How often, then, do we fail to make the effort to go just a little deeper, missing out on getting to know what they like, how they think, and essentially, who they are? How many of us feel the way this young man has felt? How many of us feel as if no one is interested because they don't make an effort to get to know who we are? Everyone has something to say. Everyone has something to offer.

When we simply take the time to ask and listen, even a few minutes, we can be wonderfully surprised about whom we meet and what they have to share. Who knows what might be revealed in the process. Who knows how you might help someone simply by showing that you care.

Who would guess that connecting with another human being, like this young man, could help everyone—including us—feel more alive?

Shame

Anything mentionable is manageable.

—Fred Rogers

That which is most personal is most universal.

—Henri Nouwen

. . . .

"What we need to do is reintroduce more *shame* into society."

When the government official stood up to share about what he perceived as the historic breakdown of the family unit and uttered those words about shame, we were astounded. It was in the midst of a monologue in which he was expressing his opinion that there aren't enough repercussions in society "about the bad things that people do." He said that by creating a culture of shame, where "deadbeats and scumbags" (his words) are reprimanded and called out for their mistakes, they would stop doing destructive things and making continually "bad" choices.

At that, we looked at each other, and one after the other, we whispered, "That's not true! I don't agree!"

"Yeah. Neither do I. Not at all!"

We both vehemently felt that this man's approach was not the right one. The next day we blogged about it.

A few days later we were interviewed on our local public radio station, and the interviewer pressed us about the concept of shame. He had just read our blog post "Shame and the Breakdown of Society."

Later that afternoon, as the manifestations of what we were asked about shame during the interview continued to occupy our discussions and minds, we received an email from a woman with the subject line "Self-Hatred and Shame." It said,

> I sat in my car with tears in my eyes this morning listening to the entire interview … I'm at a very bad point in my life and have tried unsuccessfully to get an appointment with a counselor that I can afford. I'm a widow who has been living alone for 15 years. Each day I struggle to get through what I have to do and then drink myself into oblivion every night. As I review my life, I can show that every single thing I've done has been wrong. Every single thing. And now I'm getting older, watching friends die, and can't bear the thought of my life going on like this with such hopelessness. I'm not suicidal—just desperate for some relief from the loneliness and heaviness that I live with. You are probably being inundated with contacts … but if at some point you could contact me, I would appreciate it.

We immediately responded.

> … Thank you so much for reaching out to us. Your words touched our hearts and we want you to know that your story is very important to us. It takes a lot of strength to reach out like you did. We want to honor that and help you to find the peace, grace, hope and relief that you deserve and need …

Soon, she wrote back, "I've never told anyone else before. Never. No one."

It was hard, very hard, for her to say what she knew she needed to say. She spent a lifetime keeping it in. After decades of secrets, hiding who she was and the things she had done, she had grown accustomed to the darkness that lurked within her. It was comfortable in its own deeply uncomfortable way.

But it was time to be released from the prison she had locked herself in. The guilt. The shame. The regret. She was ready to pour it out. All of it. As much as she could. It was time for the hurt to go away. Time for amends to be made. Time for healing to begin. Time for light to shine through.

When she started talking, everything poured out. The abuse heaped upon her. The years of binge drinking. The lying. Sneaking around. Betrayals. The anger and disappointment she caused her family and friends. The lost years, too many to count. She hated them all. She relived them day after day, night after night. She hated herself for the anger and disappointment she caused, for the lost years.

But in telling it, a lock was turning inside her, and freedom was coming.

> I've decided that initially I would like to just communicate via email. I'm not sure if it will even go any further than that. I decided against Skype to start because the things I have to say are so awful and I've never told anyone most of it. I think I would try to make you like me on Skype, and if I did that, I would not be able to tell the truth. I've tried writing all these things down before, but it does no good to just tell it to myself ...
>
> I'm terrified of putting all this in writing for someone else's eyes. But it is so ironic that I found out about you now, because this is something I need so badly now at a time when I'm doing a great deal of self-examination. Thanks again for your patience with me ... I have to tell you I'm afraid. I was going to just tell you about my life,

but I realized that in doing so, I would be trying to show you all the reasons that I am such a failure. So instead, I'll just tell you what I feel guilty about. And "guilty" is a mild word …

I'm rambling. I guess it is an outlet for me to just be able to write these things down that have never, never been written. And then to send them to someone, instead of just deleting them …

I know I'm being punished. In fact, all this depression and stuff is only a part of the punishment I know I'm due …

My father used to tell me how stupid and lazy and clumsy I was. I always wanted to be a dancer, but to this day, I am unable to learn dance steps …

On and on she wrote, pouring it out, telling her story.

Her story and so many others like hers accurately describe many in today's society who feel as if they cannot share their true insides, their real selves, because of the judgment they receive, the condemnation, and the harsh words that cut them off and close them down. People can't heal if they don't first reveal.

"Your caring means the world to me. I'm hoping that I may be entering a period of peace after a few really awful weeks. The sun is shining, it is warm and pretty outside and such a day has to give one hope," she wrote.

One of our spiritual idols is the late Fred (Mr.) Rogers. He used to say, "It's impossible not to love a person if you know their story."

We shared that quote with her. We shared it to let her know that there was nothing she could say to us that would make us love her any less. Her value is not wrapped up in the mistakes she's made or the shame she feels. Her value, instead, is in her humanity and the simple fact that she is alive and here on this earth. Here for a purpose. Here to have meaning. Here to love and be loved. Shame does not help her to feel loved, nor does it help her to love more fully and deeply. Shame only makes her—and most of us—feel unworthy and unloved. Shame, instead of motivating us to "do better," usually causes us to give up, to try less, and to wallow in our humiliation. And that doesn't help us at all.

A Very Lonely Feeling

I am thankful for people who ask, "How are you?" and then make eye contact and genuinely listen to your answer! Of course, this is opposed to people who ask, "How are you?" and then while you're starting to answer, walk away or start talking to someone else.

—Wanda Jacobs

. . . .

We met with her in a local restaurant. Her husband's cancer was progressing fast. He was dying. She needed to talk.

She offered to buy us tea on that cold winter's afternoon, and it warmed us as we visited. But her spirit and outlook warmed us even more. We were intent on her story, her struggles, and her pain, unmindful of the people coming and going around us. For ninety minutes we listened, and at times, we laughed. She shared warm and powerful memories. She talked about how hard it was to be a caregiver for someone you love, especially during the last weeks of life.

At one point she said, "I am thankful for people who ask, 'How are you?' and then make eye contact and genuinely listen to your answer! Of course, this is opposed to people who ask, 'How are you?' and then while you're starting to answer, walk away or start talking to someone else."

Her story was like so many others we've heard; the themes of fatigue, frustration, and fear unite those on similar journeys.

People say to her, "Call if you need anything."

But she *needs them* to call *her*.

What she needed was someone to listen. She needed someone to tell her story to—and that's what we offered.

She spoke of what it was like to watch her husband, of more than forty years, grow weaker every day. She talked about what life would be like after he died. She pondered some of the questions confronting her. Would she continue to live where she does now? Would her aging parents need more of her help? She spoke wistfully of things she and her husband would never do together again: sit on the beach, visit their daughter and grandchildren down south, go to church.

She spoke of her husband's funeral arrangements and how he had planned his service, to take the burden off of her. She talked about how his acceptance of death and the peace he felt was giving her strength and peace and acceptance too.

She shared stories of neighbors and friends who followed through with promises instead of only saying the words. They brought meals, stopped by to visit and pray, ran errands for her, or stayed with her husband so that she could take a few moments out of the house. We reassured her that her feelings and her fears were important and mattered. We reassured her that everything she was feeling was entirely common and normal. Most importantly, we simply were present with her, trying to walk a few steps with her on a truly difficult journey to remind her that she was not alone.

Visiting with her was a life-giving afternoon for us. Hearing her story, especially the parts she didn't freely share with others, and knowing that she trusted us with it was a true privilege.

As we listened and she shared, she began her journey to the comfort, healing, and peace that she needed and sought.

Listening well and focusing without distraction is one of the hardest—but most significant—gifts that we can give to others. Yet most of us don't do it very well. It's hard to be intentional about putting all other disturbances aside and truly concentrating on another's feelings and needs. It's hard to listen, at times, to someone else's pain and brokenness. It can make us uncomfortable and uneasy.

Yet when we listen well to another person, we are saying,

> Your pain is my pain.
> Your suffering is my suffering.
> Your sorrow is my sorrow.
> Your joy is my joy.
> Your passion is my passion.
> Your delight is my delight.

We all know the disappointment we feel when others do not take the time to listen to us, to really hear what we have to share, to enter into those very common experiences of being human. We know what it feels like to have someone walk past us when we are on a lonely road. We know what it's like to have someone "listen" but not really listen. We also know what it's like to have someone ask questions without waiting for a response.

This woman and her husband were going through a very challenging time. They were faced with a reality that was changing their lives—forever. Although they had many who cared about them, at times they felt dismissed and forgotten, a very lonely feeling.

But when someone got their pain and entered into it with them, that feeling was beyond words; it was full of grace and generosity, full of comfort and care. That is a feeling we all want to have, need to have, in our moments of distress and in our times of joy.

I Have a Voice

I've learned that people will forget what you said, people
will forget what you did, but people will never forget how
you made them feel.

—Maya Angelou

. . . .

There's a scene in the Academy Award–winning movie *The King's
Speech* in which King George VI of England has a confrontation
with Lionel Logue, his speech therapist, in London's Westminster Abbey.
King George is in the Abbey to practice the vows he must speak at his
upcoming coronation. He has struggled since childhood with a debilitating
stutter, an impediment that causes him deep embarrassment and a severe
lack of confidence in his abilities. As a result, he has great anxiety that he
will be unable to recite his vows with clarity and distinction. In a powerful
exchange the king, frustrated, implores Logue, "Listen to me."

Logue responds, "Why should I listen to you?"

The king counters, forcefully, yelling, "Because I have a right. *I have a
voice!*"

Logue, silent for a moment, says, "Yes … you do."

At that moment, King George VI, whose lifelong doubts about his ability
to use his voice to live out the historic calling that has been burdened

upon him, begins to embrace his calling and rise to the challenge it presents. Like King George VI, all people have a voice, and all people need to be encouraged to share their voices, allow them to be heard, and use them for the common good. When we, Michael and Tom, were in school, both of us dreaded seeing course requirements that indicated class participation would be part of our class grade. We knew that requirement would ultimately, drastically, affect our grade. It's not that we didn't have anything to say or contribute, but we both doubted our abilities to say it or articulate it well. We often felt as if our voices would be drowned out by the voices of those who were louder or more forceful, those seemingly more articulate and confident. However, we had teachers and professors who encouraged us to speak and write freely and use the voice that we had been given. Those teachers instilled in us a sense of worth and significance. They were teachers who planted in us the seeds of increasing confidence that would enable us to develop our voices, to share them in ways that would come to help and inspire others to share theirs too.

Michael

I remember a seminary Greek professor who, at Christmas, shared a special gift she would give me if she could.

She wrote to me: *"Θα ήθελα να σας δώσω μια φωνή, ένα σίγουρο και καθαρό. Για να έχουν κάτι σημαντικό να πει."* (I would give you a voice, one confident and clear. For you have something important to say.)

She championed me. She saw something in me that I hadn't seen in myself. She gave me a true gift that inspired me to recognize that I had a voice and the ability to articulate it in speech and through the written word.

Tom

I had a similar experience in grad school. I was taking a creative writing class called Storytelling. Very vividly, I remember writing and sharing one story, wondering whether the story was any good. Trying to hide my embarrassment, I asked to use the restroom. The professor then said that the whole class would take a fifteen-minute break. I quickly left the building hoping I wouldn't get noticed. The professor followed me outside, plopped down next to me on the park bench, put his arm around me, and said a few words in his strong Irish accent that I will never forget—words which have inspired me to this day: "You're better than you think you are."

Just like Michael's professor, he too saw something in me that I didn't see in myself. He listened, and he heard my voice. He heard my heart. He heard my passion. He heard my ability—even if I couldn't hear it myself—and he told me so. These teachers taught us that our voices have the right to be heard. As two people who, in our younger years, lacked the confidence to share our voices, it was the encouragement and graciousness of others who helped us find them. It was those gifts of encouragement that today compel us to give the same encouragement to others. Everybody has a voice. Everybody has value. Everybody has something to offer. Often, it takes someone else or a certain set of circumstances for that voice to come out, for it to be heard. We write this book to encourage your voice to come out.

As C. S. Lewis has written, "Friendship is born at that moment when one person says to another: 'What! You too? I thought I was the only one.'"

In our culture, sharing or showing our vulnerability is often seen as a sign of weakness, especially for males. It should not be that way. That's also why Michael and I do what we do, to share from our own brokenness so that others may gain strength in theirs, so that they may say, "What! You too? I thought I was the only one."

When that happens, we know the chains that bind can be broken, the darkness that descends can be pierced, and the pain of heartbreak can be soothed. Most people doubt their abilities at times. But in working together we can encourage one another, and through the "What, you too?" moments that will invariably happen, we can help drive doubts away. At one pivotal point in *The King's Speech*, Lionel Logue explains, "My job is to give them faith in their own voice and let them know that a friend was listening."

We work together for that very reason. And when we hear from others that our voices, through our writing and compassionate listening, make a difference, we are reminded to use the voices that we have been given. It is our mission to remind you of the same thing too.

Let it Be

Somewhere we know that without silence words lose their meaning, that without listening speaking no longer heals, that without distance closeness cannot cure.

—Henri Nouwen

. . . .

As we listen, the frustration is evident in her voice. It has been several years, but the pain is still there. And while her husband's death still hurts, what makes it even harder to face are the comments of others who try to make her feel better. They mean well; they really do. But in their desire to soothe her troubled soul, they say things that hurt. In their discomfort with her discomfort, the comfort they offer is misguided. They really don't understand, even when they say they do. No one can truly understand, because each relationship is unique. No two relationships are the same, because no two people are the same. None of us can know—truly know—what it's really like in someone else's shoes.

But you still have your children.
What about your job? Doesn't that help to make it easier?
You have your hobbies, and you can volunteer. That can fill the void.

Well, yes. Children, jobs, and fulfilling activities can give us joy and comfort and meaning. All of them can be good; helpful, certainly. But they do not replace. They do not substitute. They do not make the loss go away.

She wonders, *Why can't they understand that?*

She asks, "Why can't they just listen to me? Why can't they just let me share how I feel without offering solutions? Without sharing well-worn platitudes? Without trying to force the pain away? Why can't they simply listen compassionately? Offering few words? Sharing no judgments? Not trying to fix me? Just getting it out and then … letting it be?"

Just like the Beatles sang: "When we find ourselves in times of trouble …"

The words begin to play through our minds as we listen to her voice. In need of nurturing and healing, she tells of her fears, frustrations, and fervent hopes. She opens up the vulnerable places in her soul, the anxious corners where shadows cast their sinister, murky hues. The song continues to play in our minds as we try to dispel the shadows with gentle replies and compassionate understanding.

"Remembering words of wisdom, let it be, let it be …"

Sometimes, that's all we need to do; but often, stepping back and giving it over "in someone's hour of darkness" is the hardest thing to do.

Let none of us be of the mind that we can do it all, know it all, or have it all to offer. Instead, let's simply be with others until they come out of the depths of their desperation and despair. And when their night is cloudy, maybe this time we can remember these words of wisdom:

And "when their night is cloudy … Let it be … Let it be."

So that when in their weakness, in their confusion when they feel lost and brokenhearted, we can be reminded that "there *will* be an answer." But we don't have to give it. Instead, in those moments sometimes the best gift we can give is to listen and to "let it be."

Just "let it be."

Being True to Oneself

The most common form of despair is not being who you are ...

—Søren Kierkegaard

Being authentic is the ability to be true to oneself. Living an authentic life requires the ability to be true to our own wants, needs and desires and not live our lives by the opinion of others. Being authentic is the ability to make self-honoring choices and stand firmly in who we are in our core. Being true to ourselves gives us the insight and compassion to see others for who they are, not who we expect them to be. It frees us up from the judgment of ourselves and others and it gives others the freedom to be themselves as well.

—Victoria Reynolds

. . . .

Michael

When I was in eighth grade, my English class was given the assignment of writing a special book report. We could pick any book we wanted, as long as it related to one of the various other subjects we had been studying in school. Since I enjoyed history and we had recently studied the Holocaust and World War II, I chose to read *The Diary of Anne Frank*. After learning about Anne Frank's experiences hiding from the Nazis in Amsterdam, I was eager to understand this teenager's thoughts, feelings, and fears as she and her family and friends were subjected to profound indignities because of their Jewish faith.

One day, another classmate of mine—a boy—walked by my desk while I was reading her story and looked at the title of the book in my hands. "*The Diary of Anne Frank*? You're reading a book for girls."

I was stunned at his judgmental tone. His ridicule hurt. At age thirteen, my peers' perceptions mattered to me. I was embarrassed and humiliated by his scorn and mocking tone, which said to me that somehow I was less than a real male for reading a book written by a girl. At that sensitive age the implications struck me hard. I don't remember today whether I actually finished that book or if I chose another one that would be more acceptable to other thirteen-year-old boys. But I do remember the disdain my classmate hurled at me and the insecurity it fostered in me for years.

Tom

Midway through graduate school—seminary—several of my closest friends asked me, "Why don't you major in counseling?" My friends saw something in me that I was also feeling within myself. Instead of being a traditional church pastor—preaching, administrating, being an out-front leader—I was feeling an especially strong calling to concentrate on the gifts of listening actively, forming relationships, walking with others through their struggles, and creating a safe place in which they could share and unburden themselves. My friends perceived that. I listened to my friends and also sought the counsel of other significant people in my life, others whom I trusted, valued, and respected. But several of those respected people encouraged me not to change my major to counseling. They told me that it would be a terrible idea to pursue counseling. Their urging prevailed. I continued studying to become a parish pastor. Deep down, I knew that path wasn't for me. It didn't use my best gifts. It didn't give me joy. It didn't stir in me a passion to do all the things the courses I was taking were preparing me to do. Yet I followed the admonitions of those who wanted me to go in that direction. And I was unhappy.

Michael

The mocking of my eighth-grade reading choice became emblematic of many instances in which, over the years, I felt that I had to hide my more sensitive, compassionate, caring side; boys weren't necessarily encouraged to value and develop those traits.

I chose to read a *The Diary of Anne Frank* because, not only was I interested in the facts about the Holocaust and World War II, but I was also interested in how those horrendous events affected the personal lives of those who were directly involved. I cared about their internal lives, what the war did to their hearts, their minds, their souls—as well as what happened to them physically and politically. The seeds of my own calling to counsel and listen compassionately to others, to help them develop deeper relationships and deeper insights, were evident when I was growing up. But boys weren't steered in that direction, and as a result, I spent a significant portion of my life downplaying that calling.

Tom

It was a significant and defining moment when a few key figures in my life said no to counseling. They thought they knew what was best for me, and I know they were trying to help. However, as they pushed and prodded me to follow someone else's path, I had to deal with a lot of pain, anguish, and suffering over the years. Following their way caused me a lot of insecurity. I questioned who I was and who I was meant to be. I was adrift, unconfident, uncomfortable.

Unearthing Those Seeds

Those experiences, and many others like them, planted seeds of doubt in both of us. It caused us to question, at formative times in our lives, who we were and who we were meant to be. When others try to mold us into their images or into images of who they think we should be, seeds of lingering insecurity and confusion are sown. If those seeds take root, then they can have a hold that grips deeply within. Sometimes, it takes a lifetime to unearth and destroy those roots. Both of us have grown to unearth those seeds that others planted within us. A major aspect of our call together is to help others find that same freedom and permission, to unearth the poisonous roots within. Learning to stop the planting of those seeds in the first place will enable us to be the people we've all been created to be—not someone else's version of it. We want to help others say, "No. I'm not going to be something that's not me any longer. I am going to be the person I know inside I am meant to be."

It's not about making irrational decisions or refusing to listen to others' wisdom and guidance. It's about being true to what we know about ourselves. It's about knowing inside what will help us to live fulfilled and complete lives. Lives that are authentic. Lives in which we are fully who we are meant to be.

What a gift it is when each of us can learn to create that life with confidence and assurance.

Healing (Michael)

A secret spoken finds wings.

—Robert Jordan

· ·

I was sixteen going on seventeen, a high school senior. I had a part-time job a couple of nights a week and on Saturdays at my great-uncle's men's clothing store, a decades-old family business. The salary was minimum wage, for my minimum skills. I was the utility employee, doing whatever jobs needed to be done around the store that day.

My uncle was usually at the store and so was his wife, my great-aunt, and another great-uncle. But there was one more regular employee, an older man. Sometimes, on a typically slow weeknight my great-uncles and great-aunt would go home early and leave the other guy and me in the store alone.

When we first started working together, I liked him; he took an interest in me, asking questions, joking with me. He was friendly and easygoing. He wasn't an authority figure to me as my uncles and aunts were. So as I got to know him, I felt at ease working with him.

But before long I got to know him in a way that was incredibly *uneasy*. He began to tell me details about his and his wife's sexual life, inappropriate details told to a minor by a man twice his age. I was embarrassed by what he shared—uncomfortable. I was not a prude about the subject. But something about the things he shared was creepy, and it felt incredibly wrong.

Telling me, though, turned out not to be enough for him. If I would leave the customer areas to go to a storeroom to retrieve a pair of pants or to check on the inventory—usually sent there by the man—he began to follow, surreptitiously and quietly, jumping out in front of me from around a corner or behind a door. He'd laugh when I startled. I could easily take a joke or appreciate kidding around. But when it became a regular occurrence, far overdone, it too became creepy and something dreaded. Quickly, his "games" became an ever-accelerating intrusion on my dignity. When he'd jump out, he'd tickle me. He'd walk by and brush up against me, a quick touch at first, which evolved into a more lingering, fuller-body contact. I tried more and more to keep a greater physical and conversational distance between us, especially when we were alone in the store. I'd make larger circles around him when I had to go by, wouldn't turn my back to him, and was always looking over my shoulder. I'd be as quick as possible when he'd send me upstairs to a storeroom. He was slower than I. I figured if I could get in and out of a room as fast as possible he wouldn't have time to follow me and hide, lying in wait for me. I always hoped for customers to come into the store. It was much less likely that he would follow me then. He would never play any of his "games" when anyone else was nearby.

The evolution continued. He started becoming more and more inappropriate, to elicit a look of alarm on my face. When that stopped being enough for him he took it further. He delighted in scaring and shocking me. He became more physically aggressive. He'd grab my hands and tried to force me to do things I didn't want to do. Because I'd always push away, resist, he got more forceful. Jumping out from behind a row of shelves, waiting for me on the other side of a doorway, lurking around some corner, he'd grab me and start tickling me as a way of trying to intimidate me and wear me down. None of it was appropriate. I hated it all.

He kept pushing further and further, more aggressively, forcing a little bit more intimate contact.

It went on like that until the end of the school year, until I graduated and left to go to college. Every time when we worked alone together. Every slow night. When it was just him and me, I knew that some sort of intrusion onto my dignity, some sort of humiliation, would occur. I was all too wise to him sending me upstairs or to the back room, to him getting too close to me or cornering me in an out-of-the-way place. I knew what he wanted, what he would try to do. I really dreaded those nights alone together.

And I never told anyone about them. No one. Not ever. Not once. Never did I share what was going on at the store. I never told my great-uncles or my great-aunt. I never told a friend. I never told my parents. I never uttered a word about any of it, when I was sixteen going on seventeen.

I knew what was happening was profoundly inappropriate.

I was embarrassed that it was happening to me, profoundly so.

I was afraid that no one would believe me; that the other guy would deny it, of course; that I would look like a liar because I had no way to prove what was going on. A troubled kid making up fantasies for some sort of sick attention—I was afraid that's what others would think. I was humiliated that I couldn't stop it, that I felt powerless to change the dynamics of the situation. Always a small kid, I never felt as if I had any sort of ability to counter others who were bigger physically. I was ashamed that somehow, inexplicably, I might have been doing something to encourage his behavior, leading him on. I was afraid that I might lose my job, even more horrified that I might be branded within the family, be seen as depraved myself.

I didn't know what to do, what to say. So I said nothing and buried his abuse and humiliation deep inside. It was during a time and an era when little was said about sexual abuse, especially when perpetrated against a boy. Victims of sexual abuse weren't taken seriously. Often they were looked upon as having brought the actions on themselves. It was forty years ago, and a different perception prevailed.

So I kept quiet and put up with it. I didn't know that I had a choice. I was scared. I felt alone. I certainly didn't think that there was anything I could really do about it.

Today, as a grown man, a husband, a father of three, a pastor, and a counselor, I regret that silence. Today I know that I could speak up, that I should. And so I do. It's years too late. I so wish that I could have decades ago. But I write about it today, about one teenager's year of silence and loneliness, to let teenagers and any one else know that they do not have to endure abuse alone. To let them know that abuse really does happen. But that it should not. That there are others among them who also know its dread, humiliation, and shame, its scars and its effects. I tell my story so that others might know that they can tell theirs too. That they don't have to put up with it. Hold it in. Bury it deeply within. Tolerate it.

I want them to know that understanding people *will* believe them. They *will* listen and not judge. In their understanding they can convey that nothing the abused person has done has brought the abuse on or caused it to be deserved.

What I regret most is not that I didn't tell the story long ago for myself but that I didn't tell it for others. Perhaps if this man had been abusing other boys, my speaking up could have stopped him. No boy, no girl, no one should ever be threatened or violated like that.

My prayer is that the more of us who speak up, who give voice to our humiliation and shame, the more will be unveiled, the more will be understood, and the more will be stopped.

Then maybe, the more will be healed.

A Magical Life

When life gives you a hundred reasons to cry, show life
that you have a thousand reasons to smile.

—Unknown

*... yesterday was a magical day. We went to the beach
and I actually got into the ocean on one of the big bubble
wheelchairs. A great day with the family, sun and waves.*

. . . .

It was thrilling to read this message from him. A great day. Magical. He
hadn't had many of those lately. When he called to talk the day after
sending that email message, to tell us more about that magical day, his
voice was full of excitement, full of life. He was simply ... overjoyed. Life
didn't get much better. A day at the beach, outside in the sun, the fresh salt
air, the call of the seagulls, the sand on his feet, together with his family.

Life indeed was very good that day.

So it was a profound shock when we received the call from a friend two
days later. He was gone, she announced gently. He had slipped away,
quietly and peacefully, surrounded by his family.

It was unbelievable, stunning in its ferocity, the swiftness with which the
end came. So quickly after that magical day. Too soon. Suddenly.

Yet we shouldn't have been surprised. His emails, several a week, and regular phone calls, detailed a continuous decline and drastic loss of weight, mobility, and comfort. His limitations were increasing; his options, ending.

Still, when the call came that Friday morning, with the news that he was gone, that his life here was over, it was hard to believe. Just that Monday he was at the beach, floating gloriously on the water. Just that Tuesday he had written to share about that magical day. Just that Wednesday he called to talk in depth about his overwhelming joy. And suddenly that Thursday it was all over. The wonder of his magical day was still resounding. How could he be gone?

The next day, feelings of utter awe and emotion overflowed us as we stood in the dining room of his home, the room that was converted into his bedroom for his final days. It was the room in which he had died and in which his body still lay. His wife, closing the door behind her as she left, said, "I'll give you a few minutes alone with him."

It was an incredibly intimate and intense moment and very deeply moving. We were filled with gratitude beyond words—gratitude for the wisdom he shared in his life, the wisdom that can only come from a dying man who is able to see what really matters in life, of a man who understands the frailty of life and what we must do to savor life for the brief time we are here.

It was a privilege to sit in his kitchen a little later, at his family's table, with his wife and children, his father and brothers. To be invited into this intimate gathering as they shared stories of his life, his legacy, and his love was humbling. We all listened and learned. Everyone spoke of his wisdom, laughed about his idiosyncrasies, and became tearful as his absence continued to settle in. We all shared our blessed memories of him.

A unique and intimate bond had been forged between us. For two and a half years we had carried on a conversation, through email and over the phone—a conversation about his journey with cancer. Sometimes others who were on the journey were involved too. We discussed every detail, every nuance. It was an ongoing, intimate conversation.

Nothing was spared. Often, it wasn't pretty. But it was real. And in its raw intimacy, it was powerful—and sacred.

Yet with him, no matter how painful the journey was, no matter how uncertain the future, in every email, on every call, his voice never wavered. Never. He never strayed from the same message, the message that life was good. Each new day was a gift. No matter how dire his circumstances, he could find joy. There was always something to be learned from every situation. Gratitude was vital. Love was the essence of life.

He had an incredible attitude—relentlessly inspiring. He never lost those values. He never faltered at sharing wonder at the wonder in his life. Even up to the day he died, he never gave up on hope.

His last words that we remember were about his magical day, a day that was inconceivably good, a blessed gift. A day filled with deep joy. A day in which he learned that a wheelchair could float. A day for which he was profoundly grateful, and one that was defined by profound love.

The memory of his magical day serves as a symbol of a magical life, his magical life. For he lived his life, even as it diminished physically day by day, looking at each day as something special, something to embrace, and something to value. No matter what.

He taught us about being grateful. He taught us about true appreciation for what really matters. He taught us that even in the seemingly most diminished of circumstances, there can be joy. As he said so many times, "When we have nothing else left, when we are boiled down to our essence, our essence is love."

Love is all that matters. Simply love.

And it is love alone that brings meaning and worth to our lives. His life and death were examples of wholehearted living at its most inspiring, at its best. These are lessons from a dying man we pray we will never forget.

To Laugh

Someday I hope you get the chance to live like you were dying.

—Tim McGraw, "Live Like You Were Dying"

. . . .

Several years ago there was a retreat near Baltimore, Maryland, for people living with life-threatening illnesses. The time we shared together was intense, invigorating, and instructive. At the end of the week our minds and hearts were overflowing with the spirit of the good people who were there. The insights they taught about what it was like to live with a life-threatening and life-altering condition were inspiring and illuminating.

But it was a deceptively simple act near the end of the retreat that would become our strongest memory from the week.

A soft-spoken man, age forty-four, weak from his particular disease, attended the retreat with his wife, who helped and supported him physically. They lived on the sunny coast of Florida, and the January cold made it especially challenging for him. But he persevered quietly, anxious to absorb any wisdom he could as he struggled to live with his challenging circumstance.

Through the last afternoon and night of the retreat it snowed. The wooded countryside surrounding the retreat center was especially beautiful in the twilight moments that day. A stillness and calm descended outside our windows, and there was a magical quality to our final retreat hours together. During dinner that night our friend from Florida became animated for the first time that week. The snow, which he hadn't seen in years, absolutely enchanted him. He was boyishly excited to see it, feel it on his face, and delight in its splendor.

It gave him an idea.

The next morning, after our last session and as everyone began to say their wistful goodbyes, he announced that he wanted to do something he had never done before. He wanted to lie in the snow and make a snow angel. His childlike wonder at the miracle of the snow transported him back to a simpler time, an innocent time when disease did not threaten and his future was still open and bright.

We all loved his idea.

We gently helped him down into an undefiled blanket of snow, at least six inches of it, and he slowly spread his arms and legs to create an angel. As he did, for those moments, he was free. He was young. He was not in pain. He was not weak.

He laughed and laughed, loudly and exuberantly, from somewhere deep down within him. A moment of silliness was in his life again. It was a deeply needed moment of childlike fun, full of relief and release—for him and for all those living with life-threatening illnesses. His laughter transported us all. Everyone there shared in his joy.

Sadly, a few months later he was gone. His life ended too soon. But his moment of joy, of laughter, of silliness, of release, lives on. Forever.

That afternoon, when we were driving home from the retreat, a song came on the radio and brought tears. It was Tim McGraw's classic "Live Like You Were Dying."

The song starts talking about a man in his early forties who receives a tough diagnosis, one that "stops him on a dime." It causes him to reexamine his life, and instead of wallowing in despair, he feels compelled to appreciate and savor the time that he might have left. He decides to embrace the fullness of life, and most especially he sings,

> "And I loved deeper, and I spoke sweeter,
> And I gave forgiveness I'd been denying."
> And he said, "Someday, I hope you get the chance,
> To live like you were dyin'."

It might not have been skydiving, Rocky Mountain climbing, or bull riding, but that frail snow angel was our friend's moment to live. He was dying, but the new fallen snow that morning gave him one more moment to approach his life without regret.

One more moment to laugh. To live.

The Returning
Light (Michael)

If we shall take the good we find, asking no questions, we shall have heaping measures.

—Ralph Waldo Emerson

. . . .

Every year, as soon as Halloween is over, my son Matthew waits for the lights. He's been doing it for more than a dozen years. As the days grow shorter and the nights longer, as the temperatures drop and the leaves fall, he waits for the lights. He knows that they will come.

The neighbors across the street always put up a beautiful, brilliant, and tasteful light display for the holidays, and Matthew eagerly waits for them to be turned on, which usually happens right after Thanksgiving. And then, each day between Thanksgiving and until the lights are turned off in January, he waits excitedly from midafternoon on. Each day he stands by the front windows or walks back and forth between the windows and the front door, in energetic and coiled anticipation, laser-focused, undeterred, intent on the moment of their nightly illumination.

And when each evening's moment comes, you know it no matter where you are in the house. The effervescent squealing. The rhythmic clapping.

The dancing around the house, the steps staccato, loud, repeated. It's pure joy. Pure delight on his face! And it happens every single night.

He waits for the lights. During the darkest days of the year, he stands and waits. Transfixed by those lights brightening the dim, winter sky.

For all his limitations, in the world's view—his severe mental disabilities, his autism, his two-year-old mind in a twenty-six-year-old body, his inability to speak—Matthew knows something very profound: that light will shine in the darkness. No matter how dark or how long the wait, eventually and without fail, those lights will shine again. No matter how many seasons of the year without them, there will come a season when those lights will shine again. They always do.

Life brings its own seasons of darkness. Desperate, at times. Lonely. Painful. Full of fear. But despite those seasons, a new season will come, and the light will be seen again. Whatever darkness I find within and around me, I look to my son, and I remember that a light can pierce that darkness and can begin to bring beauty and joy again. In that I find great hope each day.

A Hunger for Authenticity

Our headspace is messier than we pretend, they say,
and the search for authenticity is doomed if it's aimed at
tidying up the sense of self, restricting our identities to
what we want to be or who we think we should be.

—Karen Wright

. . . .

One night we had the privilege of meeting with a men's cancer support
group. There were nine men living with cancers of the prostate,
throat, pancreas, colon, and bladder. Some had been living with cancer for
years, some for only a few months. But each was on a journey he neither
wanted nor requested.

We were amazed at how freely these men shared their stories, at how
comfortable and open they were about their experiences and feelings. They
spoke of incontinence, depression, fear, loneliness, and doubt. But they
also shared stories of humor, faith, gratitude, courage, love, and supportive
communities. They talked about what they had learned and how they had
grown since their diagnoses. There were stories about being more patient,
grateful, and embracing life more fully. They spoke of greater trust.

Then we asked, "What is one thing that you have never shared with anyone
else about your journey with cancer?"

The room got suddenly quiet. Uncomfortable. Then, one man, the newest member of the group, responded, "I am impotent. I feel like half a man. It isn't easy. I don't like it. There hasn't been anyone else I could tell."

Finally, it was out. We could see his sadness. We could feel his relief. His big secret. The fear of many men. He got it out, and now they all knew.

But the eight others did not respond to it. They didn't need to. We realized that the rest of them had already been together so long and had already shared so many of their most intimate thoughts and feelings about the cancer that had invaded their lives that they had trust. This was just another story told in a safe and trusting place.

We left impressed and heartened and continue to be even today as we reflect on that night. These men were living authentic lives, sharing their pains and sorrows; they were not covering up their messiness, their illness, or their feelings of defenselessness. They were more at peace than we imagined possible. They were brothers together in a community of support, a community that allowed them to share in safety, with honesty and with grace.

Often, it takes a life-threatening or life-altering event, like cancer for example, to cause us to think about and assess the value and meaning of our lives. Often, it takes these events to force us to face ourselves and to ask whether we are living authentically or not.

For these men, they were in a safe environment in which they didn't have to tidy up the unsavory aspects of their lives—their cancer, their vulnerability in it, the ugliness of the disease, the fear of potential outcomes, or the fact that some of them felt less than whole because of it. It's easy to be authentic when we don't have to pretend or hide. Once the secret is out, once the story's told, it becomes easier to live with it. It doesn't matter what the issue is—loneliness, a pregnancy, sorrow, guilt— whatever it is, once we do not have to keep it to ourselves, we can begin to embrace it. Once we can share it with those we can trust, we are freer, and a weight has been lifted from our shoulders.

All of us long for that kind of authenticity. But for many reasons we do not know how to find it. We are afraid of being exposed, criticized, or not being liked for who we really are.

Masks

If a man wears one mask in public, and another in private, he will soon forget which one is real.

—Nathaniel Hawthorne, *The Scarlet Letter*

· ·

There were about seventy members of a cancer support group—caregivers, survivors, people currently going through treatment—participating that Saturday morning. The theme we had been invited to speak about was hope. The audience clearly wanted and needed to be reminded about how important hope was on the cancer journey.

After the official program ended, a line of people formed to purchase a book of daily spiritual affirmations that Michael had written for those living with cancer. That time turned out to be the most touching and significant part of the morning. It was a time when those in line began to quietly tell us their stories:

> I have prostate cancer. It's been hard. But I am doing well.
> My sister has pancreatic cancer. She is scared.
> Four weeks ago I was diagnosed with breast cancer.
> I've been in remission for eight years.

As each person approached, we would look each other in the eyes. Some wanted a hug. Some just needed to share what kind of cancer they were living with; that was enough. Others needed to offer more details and go deeper; they lingered well after the others left. And all of them wanted to know that someone else cared, that they were not alone, that their stories could be heard. They had once been scared. Many of them still were. With a life-threatening diagnosis, fear comes fast and with intensity. They chose to face their fears and come together to talk about them. They chose to open up with one another about what it was like, what it felt like, and what they were facing. Their openness was profound. It can have a remarkable healing power. Rather than run from their fears, they embraced them, and in that embrace they were finding hope.

We spoke with a man once who, when talking about his condition, refused to say the word *cancer*. He was only willing to call it *C*, as in saying, "I have *C*." He couldn't bring himself to say the actual word. It was as if by voicing it, by directly calling it was it was, it made cancer real, true. It was as if by not saying the word *cancer*, he could deny its existence and its effects.

We knew of another family whose son had AIDS. The stigma attached to that disease and how he probably had contracted the disease was too much for them to bear, so they called it cancer instead. They denied the reality of what he actually was living with and who he actually was, a gay man. Their denial left a son who ultimately died being unable to openly share who he was with his family, friends, or community. He lived inauthentically, unable to find the true support he needed in his final days—or any of his days. How sadly true that is for many of us.

The challenge we have can be life-threatening such as cancer or AIDS; it can be an addiction, a problem with anger, being stuck in a career that brings no joy, living in a marriage that is emotionally adrift, a profound loneliness that we cannot overcome. Whatever it is, as long as we hold it in and do not feel free to share it, to give voice to it, to open up about it with those whom we can trust, we will carry burdens that will crush us with the weight of their load. To the end of our days those burdens will linger.

If we are constantly afraid of what others might think, of how they will react, or whether they will judge us, we will never be true to them or, most importantly, true to ourselves. We will never be our best and genuine selves—truly contented, truly at peace, truly free—if we do not or cannot be authentic about our strengths and our vulnerabilities, about our joys and our sorrows. That weight is too heavy for any of us to bear alone. It will bury us, cripple us, and break us.

Yes, the world often tries to corral us into ways of thinking and acting and being that are not true to who we really are. Yes, it can be very difficult to acknowledge just who we really are, weaknesses and all. Yes, we are incredibly practiced at putting on masks, building up walls, and creating pretty facades that hide our true motivations and selves.

But if we could start to be open with those whom we trust, just maybe the road toward authenticity and freedom will become a little easier to travel.

The Bar

I've never been really great at trusting anybody, just because of the way I grew up.

—Adewale Akinnuoye-Agbaje

. . . .

He needed someone to tell it to.

We had no idea who we were meeting or what he needed to share. A mutual friend accompanied him to meet us late that afternoon. He wasn't comfortable "going to an office or seeing a counselor." But he was willing to meet two guys at a bar for something to drink. So we met him where it was most comfortable and most safe for him, wanting to make it as easy as possible for him.

After about fifteen minutes of the usual small talk—How are you? Do you come here often? Where do your work?—he opened up without our prompting. And for the next hour we heard his life story.

His was a saga of multiple marriages and divorces, a debilitating workplace-acquired disability that prevented him from working and kept him in poverty, chronic lung disease, and anguished family deaths, including an infant son as well as a murdered brother, that contributed to decades-long family dysfunction. He was not an old man; he was only in his fifties. But he looked much older than his years—and for good reason. Life had been harsh on him. It had taken an astonishing physical toll. Yet once he got started, it was obvious to us that he desperately needed to share, to unburden himself of what he had been carrying for so long. His story moved us. We marveled at how anyone could live his experiences and still keep going every day. We were grateful to his friend who encouraged him to meet us and who accompanied him that late afternoon.

She whispered that it was a miracle he was even there. Until the moment he walked through the door she didn't know if he would actually meet with us.

But on that afternoon he poured out decades of long-held grief, disappointment, and pain. He shared thoughts and feelings he had never talked about before. His stories weaved together to form an overwhelming saga of a crushingly challenged life. He desperately needed that release.

We meet a lot a lot of people living with devastating circumstances like this man. Each one's story is unique. Yet each one's need is the same: they need to share those stories. Many people need someone in their lives to tell it to—whatever the *it* may be. People need someone with whom they can tell their stories. They need a safe place and safe people who will listen. A place without judgment. Without condemnation. Without fear. They need others they can trust and who will help them dissipate the darkness by creating an opening for light to shine in.

Coming Home

I would rather walk with a friend in the dark, than alone in the light.

—Helen Keller

. . . .

We accompanied a friend home from the hospital. It was a journey that took two plane flights and twenty-four hours of driving through ten states. He was in a dark and lonely place. Addictions and crushing mental health challenges caused him and his family considerable anguish and distress over the years. He had been trying to manage his demons in a variety of ways. When he hit rock bottom, he sought help, but his hospital stay was rocky and ended badly. He needed to return home to seek new treatment, new therapies, and new professionals to help him heal. For three and a half days we listened.

His situation was heart-wrenching. His fears were profound. His pain was overwhelming. His hope was diminished. His connection to others was barely alive. He struggled with grave uncertainties. He felt awash in deep darkness. His joy was gone. His dreams were shattered. He feared his future was, at best, destined to be filled with more anguish, more distress, more brokenness. It was an unending cycle. He wondered, *Will it—can it—ever end?*

At times, we felt helpless and inadequate to provide comforting responses for all the questions he raised and the statements he made:

"Tell me there's hope."

"Nothing helps. Nothing. Nothing."

"I can't do this. I just can't."

"No one understands."

"I've messed it all up."

"I'm worthless. I don't have it in me to face this anymore."

In addition to anguished questions and statements of despair there were long periods of silence too, and sometimes there were profane outbursts filled with anger, despair, and guilt. We spent hours in the car, thoughts racing through our minds, with our friend whose distress was drenched in a flood of anxiety that weighed like concrete on his chest. His wife, who waited for us at home, was ready, eager, and desperate to talk when we arrived. She had a few intense, short bursts of conversation with him and several long, deep, and searching conversations with us. She was hurting too.

While there were no easy answers, no simple responses for making our friend's life whole again, there was something we could do. It began by simply making the journey home with him. We sat with him, drove with him, were silent with him, and listened to him when he cried out. We reassured him and allowed him to hold on to us. We held him back and told him that we loved him—and we meant it—even when he made it hard to love him. We prayed for him when he asked. And we acknowledged his doubts when he declared that God must not be listening.

Most times simply being present in the pain is the best thing we can do when someone is in trouble, feeling alone, and afraid. Walk with them through their darkest valley, and accompany them back home again.

Sanctuary

Don't walk behind me; I may not lead. Don't walk in front of me; I may not follow. Just walk beside me and be my friend.

—Albert Camus

. . . .

A couple of summers ago, we drove with a friend to Washington, DC. He had wanted to visit there all his life but had never had the opportunity. We spent the whole day, just the three of us. We allowed him to set the agenda to do and see all the things he desired.

That day was important to him, and because it was important to him, it was important to us. You see, for most of his life he's been analyzed by others. Counselors and therapists have pushed and prodded him since adolescence, trying to fix what they deemed to be his problems. He believes their prying caused him to internalize his challenges and prompted him to put up more and more walls between him and everyone else in his life.

At the time of our Washington trip, our friend worked in an environment in which people came to him with their own challenges, problems, and struggles. He is a sensitive, caring listener. Most likely, the challenges of his youth gave him compassion and empathy. But as one who was expected to guide others through their dilemmas, he didn't feel he had a trusted outlet to share his.

On both ends of the spectrum—as a person who has his own needs to share and as one with whom others regularly shared—he didn't have a safe, nonjudgmental place to open up. He felt trapped and uncertain of where to turn. He was lonely and admittedly scared.

When our day was coming to a close, he wanted to get a photo of the three of us in the city. We asked someone to take it, and as we posed, with him in the middle, he reached out and put his arms around both of us. That was incredibly significant. A breakthrough, actually. A true moment of vulnerability. It was his way of saying, "I really trust you guys."

How did that trust develop? Our presence showed that we truly cared about him. It's easy to pinpoint the moment when we first realized he was beginning to trust us.

It was extremely hot that day. The sun beat down on the city streets, and we were anxiously looking for a cool place to get out of the humidity and heat. As we walked by a historic downtown church, we saw that the building was open to visitors. We each like historic buildings and admired the architecture of that church.

"Let's go in and take a look around, get out of this heat, and rest for a few moments," one of us said.

We stepped into the sanctuary. It was refreshingly cool and a welcome relief. It was also refreshingly quiet. The building's thick walls and its magnificent stained glass windows blocked out all the sights and sounds from the noisy street outside. We felt as if we were in a cocoon, a peaceful, placid place. The rest of the world was safely pushed away.

For several minutes, the three of us sat there quietly, soaking in the cool, listening to the quiet, and resting our tired feet. Then, breaking the silence, our friend nearly inaudibly whispered, "I can't go back. I don't want to go back. I'm not ready to face them again."

"Can you tell us why?"

For the next half hour he did. Pouring out his heart, tears in his eyes, he told us of his searing aloneness and of his penetrating need for a change. He spoke of the supervisors who, he believed, were against him at work and who seemed to be looking for ways to get rid of him. His account of the stinging isolation of his everyday life was painful for us to absorb. We felt intensely saddened by his suffering.

He was scheduled to leave for home, several hundred miles away, in two days. His desperation to avoid returning was palpable. It was not easy to know what to say to him. How to help. How to give him our support.

So we simply listened. We sat beside him and gave him permission to reveal his pain. We sat in that sanctuary for as long as he needed. Nothing else mattered in those moments. The day's agenda could wait. Sanctuary was what he needed, a respite from the hurt he carried inside.

Without words, we said to him, "We will walk with you here today; sit with you here too. Simply walk with you and sit by your side to show you that you are not alone—and that we aren't either." Isn't that what all of us need, anyway? Someone beside us as we try to find our way?

Questions

In times of stress, the best thing we can do for each other is to listen with our ears and our hearts to be assured that our questions are just as important as our answers.

—Fred Rogers

I have a lot of faith. But I am also afraid a lot, and have no real certainty about anything. I remembered something Father Tom had told me—that the opposite of faith is not doubt, but certainty. Certainty is missing the point entirely. Faith includes noticing the mess, the emptiness and discomfort, and letting it be there until some light returns.

—Anne Lamott

. . . .

"It has been 10 months and 2 days since the worst day of my life," she wrote.

In the ten months and two days since her son's death she had been writing to us weekly, sharing some of the most poignant and searing words of grief and longing that we have ever read. Ten months and two days had passed, and the pain hadn't eased at all. In some ways it had become more intense.

She was a faithfully religious woman. In one message she wrote that she thought she had done "everything right." She attended church each week, studied the Bible, sent her children to religious schools, and raised them rooted in the faith. Her belief in God and God's power and providence were foundational elements of her life. But her son's tragic death in an automobile accident shook every one of her beliefs to the core:

> I try to cultivate my faith back but I am against the wall. I believed that God could and would heal my son. That God would give me beauty for the ashes. That God would give me double for my trouble and make up for the time that we had lost when my son was going through his challenges. And instead He took him. So either I believe that God exists and totally did the worst thing to me, took my son, didn't answer my prayers, didn't honor the faith I had. Or I believe that God doesn't exist and I have lost my son forever. What if all this time I instructed my son to believe in something that was no more than an Easter Bunny—something to make us feel good but doesn't exist? What if I led my son to believe in something that doesn't exist?? Brought him up to believe in a fairy tale and now all that was promised to him even in his religious school does not exist? He trusted me. What if I led him wrong?
>
> I have always been a person of strong conscience. Sometimes now I wonder who cares? Except for not wanting to hurt people, what really does it matter? I always wanted to honor God and please Him. But, why? He clearly doesn't answer my prayers anyway if He exists, so what is the point?
>
> Then I allow myself to flip to the other side, though not often. What if God and Heaven really do exist and my son is there? He would be looking down thinking 'Mom stop this, don't blow it now, I am here and I am well. Just

believe'. The pain that comes from thinking it isn't true is brutal and so my mind pushes it all out and I try to focus on some task at hand, which is why I have not written much lately. SO much pain.

I attended my brother's birthday party and there was a young boy, about 8 years old. He wouldn't talk to anyone, but he took a liking to me. His actions and energy and the way he spoke reminded me of my son. He looked right into my eyes and spoke and after about 15 minutes I could no longer hold back the pain and the tears. I quickly excused myself to the restroom and sobbed. I miss my son. He is not here anymore to remember old moments together, to cherish memories, to talk with about the future.

So many of the people we hear from, especially those who are hurting deeply, are asking these same questions.

"Is there a God?"

"Why doesn't God answer me?"

"How can God let this happen?"

These are age-old questions that most of us ask at one time or another, when life beats us down.

But honestly, even though we, Michael and Tom, are both trained in theology and have studied many authors and philosophers who have grappled with these very questions, there are times when we just don't know what to say to someone in such profound pain.

Sometimes—most times, actually—all we can do is what the theologian Henri Nouwen has written:

> When we honestly ask ourselves which person in our lives means the most to us, we often find that it is those who,

instead of giving advice, solutions, or cures, have chosen rather to share our pain and touch our wounds with a warm and tender hand. The friend who can be silent with us in a moment of despair or confusion, who can stay with us in an hour of grief and bereavement, who can tolerate not knowing, not curing, not healing and face with us the reality of our powerlessness, that is a friend who cares.

In light of that, this was our response to her message about God:

Thank you for once again being so open, honest, and vulnerable with your feelings and pain. You express very touchingly what you are experiencing. Your words are poignant and, as always, achingly profound. We always need time to absorb them when you write. You express such deep, penetrating meaning. You are not afraid to explore the most real of emotions, and neither do you shy away from asking the most insightful questions. We simply want you to know that your questions are incredibly astute. They are exceptionally common questions, ones that most people in such deep pain and longing also are moved to ask. But you have a way of asking that is both raw and eloquent at the same time. You are harnessing your pain and your doubts, and you are trying to find meaning in all of this, meaning that will ultimately bring you comfort and peace.

There are no simple, easy answers to your questions. Perhaps the answers begin to come in the wrestling, in the search, in the making the hard journey through the pain. By acknowledging it, by giving voice to it, by getting it out in the open, you shed more light with each new question, diminish the darkness little by little, demystify this horrific place of existing that has been forced upon you. And maybe, just maybe, in doing that you will begin to see pieces of this anguish fall away.

To us, God, above all else is love. We look at the world and all its pain and wonder too, *What is God's role in all of this?* The thing that we most cling to (perhaps the only thing, really) is that God is simply love. Love that binds us together. Love that keeps those whom we cherish in our hearts and souls forever. Love that forgives our humanness (and even embraces it). Love that lives on in your son's daughter. Love that brings you glimpses of comfort and peace in some way each day. Love that allows you to question and be angry and doubt and acknowledge your utter disappointment. Love that … (you fill in the blank). Love. God, above all, is simply love.

It is our constant prayer that this love will continue to carry you through this darkness, this prison, until you are set free again. We want to reassure you that we uphold you in our prayers together constantly. We pray that love will be your answer and your release.

Keep writing. Your words are profound expressions of love, and they need to be shared. They will surely be an integral part of your saving grace. When you are ready, the healing will come.

All any of us can do is to keep asking those questions that are in our hearts. So much of this life brings us mystery. There rarely are simple, trite answers. Platitudes never really help. To stop questioning and wrestling means to stop believing in any kind of hope. It means to stop having faith. And faith is defined as believing in something that we do not see.

Many times, the best thing we can do is to encourage each other to keep asking, to keep questioning, to keep prodding when life is so uncertain. When we do, we ultimately allow healing to take place.

Grace

I'm afraid to show you who I really am, because if I show you who I really am, you might not like it—and that's all I got.

—Sabrina Ward Harrison

I do not understand the mystery of grace—only that it meets us where we are and does not leave us where it found us.

—Anne Lamott

. . . .

In the classic story *The Phantom of the Opera*, the title character hides for years in the Paris Opera House. When he is discovered, he is wearing a mask to hide his face. The audience eventually learns that the mask hides a hideous deformity about which he is embarrassed and ashamed. He hides behind that mask because he believes that no one could ever bear to look at him, accept him, or love him. When he is finally unmasked, he discovers that there is someone who can bear to look at him, who accepts him, and who even begins to love him. He has never experienced any of that before, not even with his own mother.

At times, we all wear masks because we too live in fear. Our masks hide who we really are because we are afraid that, like the Phantom, we will not be accepted or loved. We fear that if others saw us as who we really are they would reject us. We fear that we are not attractive enough or successful enough or smart enough or good enough to be lovable. So we put on facades.

We met a man, and initially, he wouldn't allow us to see his face. But after a few weeks of sharing he began to trust us. He began to open up and show us, and the world, who he really was. His mask began to come off.

He reached out to us from halfway around the world. We were very humbled by the connection and amazed at how social media could be utilized for good in this world. A friend had referred him to us, and we connected through Skype. While he didn't want us to see his face, he wanted to see ours. He needed to see our reaction when he shared what he needed to share. In his thick African-accented English, he asked, "You guys talk a lot about grace on your website and in your writing. Can you tell me a little about what you mean by grace?"

He was feeling us out. He needed to see and hear firsthand what we believed and how we lived out our values.

Would these two guys respond, as so many have done throughout my life, with judgment, criticism, and a lack of understanding and empathy? Would these two cower when I told them the truth about my life? Or would these two genuinely show me love and acceptance despite the choices I have made?

We went on to share, during our first few meetings, about grace.

"Grace," we explained, "is about seeing everyone as being lovable, worthy, and human. We all have something to offer. We all need to be heard. We all have a story to tell. We all have made mistakes but are always learning what it means to be human. We are all learning what it means to be loved for who we are, what it means to love others the way we need to be loved, and the way to love ourselves despite our limitations."

We went on to remind him, in those early Skype conversations, that there was nothing that he could ever say or do that would make God not love him or make us not love him either.

He continued to describe his situation:

> Imagine a state of emotional pain, guilt, and condemnation coupled with frustration and anxiety. Imagine uncountable unsuccessful attempts to overcome a number of sexual habits which are regarded as shameful and abominable by culture and society. Same-sex attraction has been my struggle since my teenage years. I have struggled with pornography for more than a decade. The feeling of "I wish I was never born" is always constant in my mind. I never told anyone about my struggles for fear of being ridiculed and rejected. I live with pain and a sense of failure.
>
> I have made several commitments and rededicated myself to God to live a life of sexual purity. To sustain this, I prayed and fasted. At times, I would feel like I overcame my struggles, because I had gone through several days without engaging in some practices. It was like fighting "weakness" with the grit of my teeth. I broke my own commitments and promises several times. Then, I felt guilt and condemnation. The more I tried, the more I failed, and this cycle has continued for several years. I was in control and playing the game of self-righteousness. It was willpower and the tyranny of fear at play. I was enslaved. I hated myself.
>
> I was enslaved by fear. Fear would tell me, "If you don't straighten up and quit watching unlawful pages on the Internet, the authorities will find out, and you will face the full force of the law." This scared me to death. Over

and over again I made the same commitments to myself and God. I broke those promises again and again.

I learned about grace and unconditional love from a grace-preaching ministry. It was a great message, or at least that's what I thought for many months. My intellectual understanding of the message was that I was perfect, holy, sanctified, and accepted before God. I had never heard a message like that. But the good news came with a condition. I needed to meditate on the Word of God, the Scriptures, day and night. I needed to renew my mind with the Scriptures. I needed to plant the seed of the Word of God in my heart. I needed to quit "making mistakes." I needed to uproot the bad seeds and start planting the seed of the Word of God in my heart. I embraced this message with my whole heart and never had any idea that it would plunge me into more pain, frustration, and legalistic religious obligation and bondage. I tried it for several months but struggled with the same challenges over and over again.

It was clear to us that he felt ashamed and betrayed. He was confused and hurting. He didn't trust us. He was initially skeptical of our different message about grace, not understanding that it didn't come with conditions or requirements. He didn't believe that we would accept him for who he was, struggles and all. He didn't believe we could love him, because he had been told he was unlovable.

We shared a message of love and friendship and tried to converse in a nonjudgmental tone. We told him, "It's okay to struggle. It's human to be vulnerable. We are not in control. We don't have the power to transform our lives by ourselves. Having a bad habit does not mean you have the power to fix it on your own. You are not alone. You are a child, and God is the Father. God never sees you a failure."

In another conversation, he told us that he was learning to be free and learning to let go of the illusion of control. He said he no longer pretends that he can fix his struggles alone. He recognizes that God wants him to depend on him. It was astonishing to him that we accepted him.

He said, "I still have no idea how you know so much about me and yet accept me the way I am!"

We all want to show the world who we truly are. When we have the freedom to remove our masks and be who we are with people we trust, our lives can be so much richer. It is liberating to shed our shame and share our fears and to ultimately learn that we are not alone.

Worthiness Is Our Birthright (Tom)

In every aspect of our lives, we are always asking ourselves, "How am I of value? What is my worth?" Yet I believe that worthiness is our birthright.

—Oprah Winfrey

. . . .

I can count on two hands the number of times I've cried as an adult. Earlier that day was once. I had a strange feeling inside my gut that it was the beginning of the end for me. I was scheduled to meet with my supervisor later that morning so we could discuss my future at the church.

Things hadn't been going well for a long time. The problems actually started my second day on the job, when she walked into my office and laid it out for me: "There are two camps here. You need to choose which one you want to be in. You have to pick who you're going to be loyal to: me or him."

I didn't know how to respond. I was stunned at her statement. I tried to be as diplomatic as I could. She was playing me off against her supervisor. I was instantly struck with terror. *What have I've gotten myself into?*

After she walked away, I immediately called another pastor. "Is this normal at a church?" I asked him.

He responded with disbelief and was as alarmed as I was.

Many moments like that one followed. None of them felt right to me. Whether it was the church sexton who criticized me for not keeping the youth room clean enough, the office administrators who wouldn't relay messages for me when I was working outside of the office, or the people who tried to undermine my authority and questioned my competence, there were always fires to be put out. Those fires made it increasingly difficult for me to do my job—caring for the members of the church. All of that and more served to increase the doubts I had about my worth.

Why would people in a church act this way? Why would people anywhere operate like this?

It was my first position out of graduate school, and I didn't know what to expect. Yet two years later, when I cried and waited to be called into her office, I knew exactly what to expect. I expected that it wasn't going to be good, and it wasn't. For two hours she told me everything I had been doing wrong. There seemed to be absolutely nothing that I was doing right. I felt like a complete failure. A disappointment. Incompetent. Useless.

Halfway through the meeting I started crying. Again. Twice in one day. Embarrassed, I asked if she could close the door.

"No. I can't do that."

I wasn't even given the dignity and the safety of absorbing all of it in private.

She gave me an ultimatum: change everything I'd established and do things a different way—or get out. Intellectually I knew that she was telling me what she had been pressured to say. These weren't her words, exclusively. This was a system-wide dysfunction. But my heart was broken by those words. Reeling and despondent, I stumbled home, propelled by a force that wasn't my own. I felt utterly worthless.

I had already been struggling. I didn't know if I really wanted to be a pastor in a church. This just confirmed my internal struggle. As I went toward home, I confirmed the thought that I literally had nothing to offer. Now I knew for certain that I was no good. I felt worthless and insignificant. I felt horrible about myself, and that is something I hope I never feel again.

When I got home, I climbed the stairs and went straight to bed, pulling the covers over my head. In my cocoon I desperately ached for the world and its pain to go away. I lay there, still and numb, most of the rest of the day.

I have never entertained suicidal thoughts, but in those hours I could empathize why someone could feel that way. When you feel as if your life is wholly worthless, it could be incredibly easy to simply give up.

But out of our deepest pain and hurt and brokenness there can come goodness and redemption and release.

Through it all Michael and a few others reminded me of my worth. When it seemed as if no one else cared, they saw goodness and value in me. Michael played a role of encourager, affirmer, supporter, and cheerleader. His presence was exactly what I needed during that time. He constantly reminded me, with his words and especially by listening with patience and compassion, that my life was of worth and of value. He reminded me that I possessed inherent gifts that were meaningful, useful, and needed. His unwavering presence showed me that I had something great to offer.

In that, there were glimpses of what would become Someone to Tell It To today.

Every one of us is scared about something, maybe about many things. Every one of us feels unworthy at times. Every one of us fronts a facade that masks our inner demons and uncertainties.

It is a foundational element of our mission today to remind everyone of their worthiness, to listen intently and patiently enough to go beyond the surface, and to shed light on the deeper truth of others' souls.

I needed that from Michael, and he gave that to me. Today we give that to one another, literally every day. We remind one another of each other's worth and significance in this life. And now together we do that for others around the world who need to be reminded too. It's human nature to ask oneself, *How am I of value? Does my life matter?*

Together, Michael and I believe that worthiness is our birthright. Our mission is to take that message, one person at a time, to the entire world.

Over Time (Michael)

Certain stories we carry with us, events in our life, they define who we are. It's not a matter of getting over anything; we have to make the best of it.

—Nick Flynn

. . . .

I remember vividly my first day as a pastor. Just having graduated, I was assigned to serve a small rural parish. The moving van had just been driven away, and we were left with our oldest sons, nineteen months and two months of age, in the midst of the chaos of unplaced furniture and unpacked boxes. We didn't know where to start. It was overwhelming.

A knock came at the door, and standing on our front porch was a prominent and formidable church member. I greeted her and invited her in. She stayed on the porch. With barely a hello and without a warm welcome, she proceeded to let me know in no uncertain terms who was boss in this parish; it definitely wasn't me. She went so far as to tell me how furniture needed to be placed in the house. We hadn't been in the house for even an hour, and already I felt as if my family's home and life were no longer ours. Starting on such a negative foot, I feared what would follow over the next few years. Feeling anxious and besieged, I sat down on our sofa and cried uncontrollably. I wondered too, as did Tom when he arrived at his first church position, *What have I gotten myself into? Is this normal at a church?*

At that moment I desperately wanted to run after the moving van that had just left and call it back. I would have loaded up our family and all our belongings and escaped before it was too late. But it was already too late. We had to stay. I ached for the protective cocoon of school again.

At that moment I had never felt so alone, so insecure, so reluctant to start a new chapter of my life.

If I am going to be completely honest, I have to admit that I really didn't want to be a pastor in a church. It was not something I had ever aspired to. My seminary graduation day was one of the saddest days of my life. I loved my time there. I was a coeditor of the school paper, an officer in the student government, and an active member of the seminary's performing arts group, and I had made some wonderful, close friends. My first two sons, Adam and David, were born when I was there, and I gained tremendous discipline and organizational skills in order to be a new father and a full-time student. I grew exponentially in my faith and in my ability to articulate and live out that faith. I learned how to put my faith into meaningful action. I came to believe in a God of love, compassion, and grace. That's whom I wanted to serve. I wanted to help people who were in pain, to work to show people love, compassion, and grace. I desired to walk with others on their journeys to discover those attributes for themselves.

But deep down I feared that within the walls and traditions of the church it might be painfully hard to fully live out those hopes and desires.

One experience from the church in which I grew up affected my feelings and fears about that. We had a pastor whom I liked very much. He was a gentle, kind man in his sixties. He had gone to seminary and become a pastor in his sixties, after he retired from his lifelong job. Because of a lack of money when he was a young man he had had to defer the dream he had of going to seminary. He got married, raised his children, and took another career path instead. But he never gave up on his dream.

It didn't take long after he was assigned to our church that a few members of the church let him know too who was in charge. It wasn't him. They tried to control all that he did. They criticized his preaching. They wanted a puppet, not a leader.

Their sniping, backbiting, and attempts to control him eventually began to wear him down, and he got sick, sick enough to be hospitalized for several weeks. Their pressure got the best of him. He needed to take a leave for a time. They made it torture for him.

I had never met a person more pastoral, more faithful, more suited be a pastor than he was. But a self-righteous few viewed him differently and saw to it that his time with us was fraught with tension and acrimony. That colored my views of what churches were like. Even though I felt called to pursue a seminary education and dedicate my life to service and spiritual pursuits, I always harbored deep doubts about doing it as a parish pastor.

My encounter with a self–appointed guardian of the church on my first day as a parish pastor didn't do anything to alleviate those doubts.

But over time, I determined to make the best of the situation that I was in. I worked to overcome my fears. Through sheer persistence and time, my insecurities and uncertainties melted away. Over time, as I got to know the intimidating woman who met me that first day, I actually came to see that behind her gruff facade there lingered a sensitive soul who had fears and insecurities of her own. In listening to her and observing her, I came to know her deeper self. And I grew to respect and like her.

As hard as it was at first, the seeds of Someone to Tell It To and what Tom and I do together now every day were born of those painful experiences. I saw my pastor respond with grace when he was attacked. I saw him endure and never give up. I spent a lot of time with him, despite our more than forty-year age difference. He inspired me. I wanted to show him a different way than what some others had shown him. And later, whenever I felt attacked and controlled too, I drew on his example to try to react (however imperfectly) with dignity and forgiveness. In the woman who first came down so hard on me in my first parish, I saw a caring, sensitive person when I followed my pastor's example and simply kept trying to love her the best way I could. By doing that I was sustained through those times in my career when I felt besieged and diminished by someone's unloving words or actions.

Those experiences, among so many others, molded me into the person I am today. They inspired me to walk with others when they were going through terrible times. They inspired me to work to see beyond the masks that all of us wear, to see something deeper, and to see ultimately, almost all the time, something good in everyone.

If I can do those things every day, then I am fulfilled, and I am doing exactly what I believe I have been created and called to do.

I thank God that I get to do it with someone every day who wants to do the same thing too.

Dandelions and Sand Castles (Tom)

The soul is healed by being with children.

—Fyodor Dostoevsky

I try to be grateful for the abundance of the blessings that I have, for the journey that I'm on and to relish each day as a gift.

—James McGreevey

. . . .

Several months ago, when it wasn't so cold and rainy and the days were longer, I took my four children, ages six and under, to the park. I needed a break and wanted to get out of the house.

Not only was I fretting about my fatherly responsibilities, but my children were being children. They woke up early. They ate. They pooped. They spilled milk on the carpet. They watched the same shows over and over and over again. They hurt themselves. They broke things. That's what they did; they were children.

On that particular hazy, hot, humid, mid-July afternoon I was in survival mode. I was simply trying to make it through the day without any major accidents—just waiting until my wife got home.

When I get in survival mode, I get frustrated easily when my kids are acting their age. I lose my temper when my son takes a pen and writes on the wall, instead of teaching him there are better ways to share his artistic efforts. I yell when my daughter tries to pour apple juice in her cup and spills half of the juice on the floor instead of appreciating her effort to be independent.

On my drive to the park, our local mechanic called with the news that our van needed two new tires, a new set of brake pads, and a few other parts.

"Great! Just great!" I shouted through clenched teeth. I punched the steering wheel as I thought about the cost—$500 we didn't have saved or budgeted.

It had already been a tough week with many unexpected surprises—and not birthday party surprises or Christmas morning surprises. First it was a leaky faucet. A doctor's bill in the mail. Then our lawn mower stopped working. And now a call from the mechanic to top things off.

After unloading all four children out of the van, the same van that needed a total makeover, my two oldest children started running toward the play area on the far side of the park. All of a sudden, they stopped. They squatted low, heads bent. Then they picked something up from the ground and ran back to me.

Filled with a sense of wonder and exhilaration over their newfound discovery, my daughter yelled, "Daddy, Daddy, do you like our flowers? Aren't they beautiful?"

Flowers?

I almost corrected her by blurting out, "Those are weeds," but I kept it to myself.

We continued on toward the play area. My son had his sights set on the sandpit. It had rained the day before, and there were still some puddles in it. I started to tell the children to go play somewhere else—somewhere less muddy so they would stay clean and dry for our dinner plans later that evening.

This time it was my son who yelled out. "Daddy, let's make a sand castle!"

"No, let's go play on the swings where there aren't any puddles," I mumbled under my breath.

After surviving another hour at the park, I was ready to leave. I piled all four children back in the van. A few minutes into the drive, my oldest daughter asked if we could stop at Wendy's for a ninety-nine-cent Frosty.

"No! We can't stop for Frostys, We have no money!" I shouted.

Of course, my daughter had no idea or understanding of the incredible financial weight I was feeling that day. Everyone was quiet in their disappointment.

When I pulled into the driveway, I glanced in the rearview mirror at the four beautiful children sitting quietly in the back of van. In that moment, I realized how much of the day I had missed out on and how my children were trying to show me, once again, the simple joys in life.

It's so easy to look at dandelions scattered throughout our lawns and see weeds eating up our precious green grass instead of seeing flowers or a beautiful creation. When we see a puddle in the middle of a playground, it's easy to see a potential hazard or an impending mess instead of an adventure or a possible discovery. When our children ask for a simple treat, it's easy to see a threat to our depleted bank accounts rather than a treat or a respite amid the burdens that weigh us down in life.

Children have a way of showing us simple joy, discovery, and play around every corner. Children aren't stressed about making the next car payment. They aren't frustrated because their coworker got a raise and they didn't.

They aren't overburdened with busyness. They live in the moment, and they are able to see the spiritual in the mundane, the beautiful in the ordinary.

We make life's journey so much more difficult sometimes by not sharing in our children's wonder, excitement, and joy. If we can teach ourselves to see dandelions as flowers and potential castles in sandy puddles, we could find more delight, more anticipation, more peace, more hope, and more love for the beautiful life we have been given. The journey that we share would be so much more wonderful than it's ever been before.

The Capacity for Resilience

The human capacity for burden is like bamboo—far more flexible than you'd ever believe at first glance.

—Jodi Picoult

. . . .

Widowed with three children ages seven, five, and three, her life unraveled into a spiral of turbulence, depression, and pain. Her husband's suicide changed her life forever.

We asked her how she managed, how she got through it, how she survived.

"I did what I had to do," she said.

She knew that she had to make it through for her kids. They were so young, so impressionable. They needed stability. They needed to be grounded and unconditionally loved.

She did everything she could to provide that. Her kids are young adults now, and she looks back with deep and abiding pride at the good and caring people they have become.

> For months they wanted to go to sleep with me; they needed the comfort of my presence. My bed wasn't big enough for all of us together. So for the first six months we camped out on the living room floor. We ate a lot of pizza

and any other comfort food we could find. We wore out a copy of the movie *Grease* and sang its songs over and over. We did whatever it took to make it through the difficult days and the darker nights.

I did what I had to do.

Some days I took all three kids to my parents, two blocks away. I simply needed alone time. It was on those days when I was absolutely at my wit's end. I'm grateful my parents were there. Oh, and I was so thankful too for the Social Security the children received. Without that help I don't know what we would have done.

The depression at times was overwhelming. I toughed it out. I knew those periods would end. But, wow, were they hard! Dark. Lonely.

I did what I had to do.

And now, I have the three most loving, responsible, loyal kids in the world. They're my passion and my life. I got through that time because I just didn't want to let them down.

She got through it, and today is thriving in ways she never thought possible. She did what she had to do. She is a remarkable woman. Strong. Resilient. Courageous.

She needed that strength, resilience, and courage on the day her doctor said, "I'm sending you for a CT scan for your abdominal discomfort."

Surgery followed; the tumor on her pancreas was removed. But two years later while she sat in her doctor's office, her doctor asked, "What's wrong? Why are you crying?"

Through her tears she said, "I don't want them to find another tumor, and I'm scared."

Her doctor gave her our card, and two weeks later she sat with us at a coffee shop, meeting us for the first time.

"I'm scared."

In the months that followed we met every few weeks at that same coffee shop. She shared her life's story. Her life has been hard. Incredibly hard. When she thinks about it all, sometimes she gets angry.

As a pancreatic cancer survivor fearful of the disease's return as well as living with chronic restless leg syndrome, she continues to need the strength, resilience, and courage she exhibited as a widowed single mother. Most of her nights are spent in pain and fitful sleep. She is often extremely tired and in despair about the agonizing ache of her legs.

Life's unrelenting challenges continue.

But most significantly for her, she has lived all her life with the fact that she has never followed her dreams. She has been unable to use several of her most important gifts to their full potential and has missed out on the passions they stir. There has always been something missing in her life, and she has struggled to discover as a result.

If there is any attribute that comes to mind as we listen to her, it is her resilience. She has overcome so much in her life. Tragic death. Difficult diseases. Lack of affirmation. Having to do so much on her own.

We find her strength and resilience inspiring, and yet she doesn't see herself as resilient at all; she says she was just doing whatever she had to do to get through. We see an inner resource, an innate power within her, that has guided her and seen her through life's difficulties. Some call that inner resource God; we certainly do. And it has given her what she has needed to rise above her losses, her pain—physical, emotional and spiritual—while she was so often alone.

What impresses us most is that now, at age fifty-five, she is coming into her own. She is beginning to grow fully into whom she was created to be. She is a strong, compassionate, passionate, caring, loving woman, mother, daughter, and friend.

One of her gifts is singing. She's really good—tremendous, in fact. But she wasn't given the encouragement she needed to pursue that gift. In fact, she was routinely discouraged. Recently, however, she was given opportunities to perform at local community events, stirring her long-simmering desires to share her talents. She's put together a band and a set list and is confirming more and more dates to sing. She is clearly at home when she is performing onstage. She's a different person. She's a new woman, at peace and filled with joy.

Another of her gifts is the ability to write. She has started and completed a book based on her parents' courtship during World War II, when her father was serving in Europe and her mother remained at home. She recently discovered the letters her father wrote to his waiting fiancée at home. The letters he wrote to her mom are a treasure of insight and love during war a lifetime ago. Theirs is a beautiful story, and it is life-giving for her to tell their seventy-year-old story of love and longing.

When she talks about her struggles, we can see the pain in her eyes and hear the anxiety in her voice. But when she speaks of her singing and her writing, something changes. Her eyes brighten. Her voice becomes confident and clear. We watch her body language and the way she shifts in her chair; her demeanor changes from one of carrying the world's weight on her shoulders to one of release, serenity, and joy. We watch her be transported into a different place, a more secure place, a more blissful state, as she describes what she most loves to do. She hits her stride. She is more completely herself, fully engaged in who she is and who she was born to be. That is resilience—rising above the challenges, going on in spite of the losses, stepping beyond the discouragements, and living through the pain.

Webster's Dictionary defines *resilience* as "an ability to be able to recover from or adjust easily to misfortune or change."

That's our friend. Resilient to the core. Her life has become more abundant because of her resilience.

Throughout her whole life she has neither been given the permission nor had the opportunity, based on her own circumstances, to enjoy an abundant life. We tried to do that for her, encouraging her to follow her joy, to pursue her singing and writing.

One day we received this message:

> Every time I meet with you both, I come away with a feeling of "Heck yeah, these guys get it! They understand where I'm coming from and help me to see a positive direction that I should turn to. They encourage me to keep going and pursue dreams, dreams that once seemed so unobtainable, but now they are dreams that I can reach out and touch. Dreams that already have and will become a reality."

The abundant life she has always sought is finally, deservedly, coming to her.

To Forgive (Michael)

Forgiveness is an act of the will, and the will can function regardless of the temperature of the heart.

—Corrie ten Boom

My dad is a Holocaust survivor. He survived with the help of others and through his own fierce will, anger, and bravery. As a child, I would wonder and worry about whether I'd have the personal power to survive something so terrible. I'll never forget the sense of relief his answer gave me: "Worrying about that question is futile. Don't even try to imagine how you'd handle a holocaust, because in the face of a crisis like that, you'd become someone else—someone with a strength you couldn't even picture or imagine now."

—Ken Page, LCSW

. . . .

The weather that morning—gray, gloomy, bracingly chilly—matched the atmosphere of the place we were visiting.

Dachau. The infamous Nazi concentration camp, outside Munich, Germany.

As my family and I walked through the grounds, our mood became increasingly as dark as the sky. Our spirits became cold at what we saw: the gates through which we entered, *"Arbeit macht frei"* (Work will set you free); the guard towers; the trenches; the fences ringed with razor wire; the stark barracks; the crematorium; and the burial grounds holding the ashes of untold thousands murdered there. Each was a symbol of unfathomable hatred, inhumanity, and horror.

Much of our visit was spent in silence. What does one say? How does one even begin to comment adequately or appropriately on what we saw and were challenged to remember? The museum on the grounds was almost too much. In fact, it was impossible for me to read it all, to look at all the images, each one more sickening than the next. I couldn't take it all in. The unimaginable story told there penetrated my entire being in a way that I will never be able to shake. None of us will, and perhaps we never should. Perhaps those images and our memories from that visit should stay with us. We must never forget what can happen when we allow our prejudices and our fears to overwhelm us.

One small image stood out for me above the rest. It was a frame containing the different colored "badges" or triangles that identified the reason prisoners had been detained there: yellow for Jews, green for professional criminals, purple for certain other religious believers, and pink for homosexuals. Then there was black for those with disabilities. That one hit hard. It was an intensely painful reminder that our now twenty-six-year-old son, Matthew, who lives with autism and severe intellectual disabilities, would have been one of those forced to live—and most likely die—at a camp such as Dachau.

These images, and the horrific story they so vividly tell, remain seared in my mind and in my heart.

But so is a story by Corrie ten Boom that I had read fifteen years before that visit to Dachau. Corrie ten Boom is a Dutch woman who was imprisoned at the Ravensbrück women's concentration camp in northern Germany because she and her family helped many Jews escape the Holocaust. Her story, "Love Your Enemy," is full of pain and sorrow, but it also describes the path that leads to freedom and redemption and ultimately to healing and forgiveness. It is a story that is seared just as vividly in my mind and in my heart as my visit to Dachau, and it is nothing short of breathtaking for me in its power and inspiration.

Her story takes place a few years after the war ends. It is the story of a harsh guard, before whom she had previously stood naked, vulnerable, and humiliated, and under whose watch her beloved sister, Betsie, had died. It is the story of coming face to face with this harsh guard—one of the cruelest guards she had encountered in the camp—when he comes to one of her talks after the war.

Corrie ten Boom, after surviving the camp and the war, felt led to write and speak about her experiences, how she found healing from them, and how she learned to forgive the unspeakable evil she and millions of others encountered during that time. She also reassured others that, through forgiveness, they could find freedom from whatever imprisoned them too.

It was in a church basement in Munich when one of her worst and most painful nightmares came to life. The guard did not remember her. But when he heard her say that she had been imprisoned in Ravensbrück, he felt compelled to approach her. After her talk, the guard came up to her, with his right hand extended, to greet her. He said, "Fräulein … will you forgive me?"

She froze, not knowing what to do or what to say.

As he stood before her, his arm outstretched, his hand reaching for hers, she wrestled, for what seemed like hours, with what to do. She had just spoken passionately about the need to forgive in order to move on and the need to release the pain in order to heal. But when confronted directly with a request for forgiveness, she wasn't immediately able to offer it. But she knew what she needed to do.

Mechanically, she thrust her hand into his. She writes about what happened next:

... an incredible thing took place. The current started in my shoulders, raced down my arm and sprang into our joined hands. And then this healing warmth seemed to flood my whole being, bringing tears to my eyes.

"I forgive you, brother!" I cried. "With all my heart."

For a long moment we grasped each other's hands—the former guard and the former prisoner. I had never known God's love so intensely as I did then.

Forgiveness. It is one of the most difficult things that any of us can do. But when we can give it, it is an indescribable gift. It is also a beautiful gift to ourselves. In this mission of compassionate listening, I hear it all the time. I hear the anguished cries of those who are carrying around resentment, hatred, bitterness, unresolved anger, and pain that weigh them down. These things become a burden that poisons their spirits and prevents them from finding joy in life.

I have been asked often over the years whether I am angry about my son's condition. Do I resent his disabilities? Am I bitter about his limitations and, therefore, mine, as his needs demand so much of my time? Can I forgive God for giving me this broken child and the burden his brokenness brings?

The answer is "No. I am not angry. I do not resent. I am not bitter about anything connected to my son."

I also feel no need to forgive God, because I do not in any way believe that God has given us a broken child or burdened us with him. There is no need to forgive something that I do not believe has taken place.

That is not to say I never have a need to forgive. At times, I need to forgive others—when someone makes a careless, insensitive comment about him or when someone expresses a callous attitude about what it's like to care for a child with such disabilities. Other times I need to forgive myself when I don't handle things as I'd like, when I am impatient, tired, or overwhelmed.

It is Corrie ten Boom's story about her forgiveness of a man who represents the most evil of evils of our modern history that reminds and inspires me to believe that there is no hurt, no anguish, and no act that cannot be overcome. There is nothing to keep me from finding joy and peace in this life, regardless of my challenges and responsibilities. Her story reminds me that the pain we carry within us only serves to rob us of the good life we are all meant to live.

I refer to her story often. If she could forgive as she did, I can forgive anything too.

Unbreakable (Tom)

You may encounter many defeats, but you must not be defeated. In fact, it may be necessary to encounter the defeats, so you can know who you are, what you can rise from, how you can still come out of it.

—Maya Angelou

. . . .

It's 3:03 a.m., and I am wide awake. I would prefer to be asleep. I am not a night owl by any means—you can ask my wife. But tonight, like so many restless nights I contend with each week, I am in severe pain. I have lived with chronic pain since I was a freshman in high school. I am now thirty-two years old.

I guess you could say it all started the day before my high school baseball career. My best friend and I had just finished our final workout of the offseason. It was the last day of summer, and in just twenty-four hours we would be putting ourselves on display, hoping that all those hours of physical training, hard work, and practice would cause one of the coaches to see the same talent in us that we saw in ourselves.

While waiting for my ride, my friend challenged me to a quick pickup basketball game in his driveway. After missing my first shot, I ran to retrieve the ball and rolled my ankle. Severe pain shot through me.

Moments later my mom arrived and took me to Dr. Snyder, our family doctor.

"You fractured the growth plate in your ankle," he told me.

Over the next few years, Dr. Snyder and I got to know each other on a first-name basis.

Fast-forward to my senior year. It is New Year's Eve 2000, and I am lying on a makeshift bed in my parents' living room, and it is once again the middle of the night. What was an evening filled with laughter, excitement, and wonder for most was an evening filled with sadness, disappointment, and pain for me. Just a few days prior I had undergone a major spinal-fusion surgery to try to repair a condition called spondylolisthesis. Long word short, I had stress fractures in my lower spine. During my four years of high school I had broken my ankle twice, suffered a concussion, and had now undergone a fusion surgery most people undergo as a last resort.

Fast-forward four more years. I am a senior in college, and I am once again in Dr. Snyder's office.

"You fractured your elbow," he said.

With those words my laundry list of injuries grew longer. In four years of college I had broken my elbow twice (requiring surgery both times), broken the big toe on my right foot, broken the thumb on my right hand, broken my left wrist, and suffered two or three more concussions—I can't remember exactly.

Fast-forward a decade to present day. Our family doctor is no longer Dr. Snyder. Now, I'm on a first-name basis with Dr. Wood.

"You have a condition called fibromyalgia," he told me.

Long word short, I have arthritis running through my body, which causes achiness in my arms, legs, and back.

Friends and family have humorously compared me to Samuel L. Jackson's character in the movie *Unbreakable*. He is born with a rare disease that causes his bones to break easily. He can't go anywhere or do anything without hurting himself. He too lived with chronic pain. Samuel L. Jackson is playing a movie character. I, unfortunately, am living in real life.

Truth be told, I don't like sharing about my pain. I never have. In fact, this is the first time I have ever shared it publically. So why share it? I'm sharing it because I know that there are many people out there who need to be reminded that other people suffer too. Sometimes it helps just knowing that there are others who are going through challenges also. Maybe for you it is physical pain—a tough diagnosis, a lingering injury, or another restless night of sleep. Or perhaps it's emotional pain or spiritual pain.

And if you experience any of this sort of pain, I am deeply sorry for you. My heart breaks for you. Sometimes it's nice to know that someone else cares about you in your pain and suffering. I understand, and I care deeply.

Living with pain of any kind—physical, emotional, or spiritual—can be incredibly debilitating. There are days when I would love to wave the white flag and say, "I'm done with this" or "I give up." I'm sure you have days like that too. There are days when I have literally given our couch a TKO, and I'm not a boxer.

I guess the good news is this: we have been given so many resources to help ease our despair, comfort us from our affliction, and bring hope to our situations. We have been given friends and family. There are many who love us and care about our situations; there are friends and family who consistently show empathy, grace, and compassion in our suffering.

Pain and suffering are a part of life. I wish it weren't so.

But to have others who will walk with us through our pain is a gift from God that we all need.

Craving Appreciation

The deepest principle in human nature is the craving to be appreciated.

—William James

. . . .

We received a message one day from a woman named Jane. It touched us:

> My lifelong struggle has been over not only how or why I judge others, but how and why I judge and condemn myself. For as long as I can remember, I have felt "not worthy" and "not enough" and this has broken and scarred me in every area of my life. I am struggling to evolve toward self-love and self-acceptance without judgment, so I can truly bring that to everyone I touch in my life. Thank you for your beautiful and loving perspective.

We have been amazed by the messages we receive from people like Jane who have struggled, as we all have at times, with a lack of self-worth and self-love. It is a constant problem in our world—so many of us do not believe that we are lovable, worthy, or inherently good.

Why is it so hard to love ourselves or to accept who we are? What compels us to believe that we are broken people, broken beyond repair? Why do these scars, as Jane refers to, cover our lives and spirits?

100

Why is it such a struggle to accept ourselves without judgment?

Prior to a television interview we had, before the cameras began rolling, one of our interviewers said something profound: "Our culture tends to focus on our weaknesses, instead of focusing on our strengths. What you are trying to do is help people see and live from their strengths."

She was exactly right. That is exactly what we are trying to do. The cultural tendency to concentrate on our faults, failings, and weaknesses permeates our spirits and minds and creates in us a culture of judgment and denunciation. That tendency rarely encourages us to change ourselves or our behavior. But it instead causes us to sink deeper into a pit of loathing and despair.

It is our mission to help others to move away from that perspective, out of that pit, and to discover a better way to live. It is to share the message that everyone deserves to know that they are loved, that everyone is worthy, that everyone has something of value to offer to this world.

In his popular book *Now Discover Your Strengths*, Marcus Buckingham writes:

> Unfortunately, most of us have little sense of our talents and strengths, much less the ability to build our lives around them. Instead, guided by our parents, by our teachers, by our managers, and by psychology's fascination with pathology, we become experts in our weaknesses and spend our lives trying to repair these flaws, while our strengths lie dormant and neglected.

Instead of being experts in weakness, we strive for everyone to become experts in living a life in which we all know that we are valued and appreciated.

When that innate hunger is satisfied, just imagine how much more joyful and peaceful this world could be.

We attended a seminar in which the keynote speaker was David P. Reinhardt. Reinhardt's presentation was entitled "Arctic Insights: Learning from the Pack about Leadership and Life!" He spoke about his deep love for Alaskan husky dogs and Alaska itself. He shared how he has traveled in the state extensively and has participated in the classic annual Alaskan sled dog race, the Iditarod.

One point Reinhardt made during his presentation resonated strongly with both of us. He started describing each of the huskies on his team and what his dogs have taught him about life and leadership. As he spoke about each one by name, he listed each one's most special attributes—such as one's energy, another's patience, another's stamina, and another's sense of direction. He also listed each of their other individual characteristics—such as one being easily distracted, another aloof, another a bit skittish, and another's nervousness.

When Reinhardt described each husky, he didn't discuss their strengths and then say, "*But* here are his weaknesses. Here are her flaws." Instead, he said, "These are his strengths, *and* these are other aspects of her personality." It was subtle. But he spoke volumes with his choice of words. Reinhardt wasn't saying that the dogs had their weaknesses. He was saying instead that they simply had unique and different characteristics from one another. He was saying that each dog was unequaled, that each dog offered distinctive attributes that added something valuable to the team. He was saying that each dog had gifts that were important and that mattered.

Reinhardt's message about the dogs *and* about us as humans in leadership and life included the following points:

- Every individual has pros and cons.
- Your pros and cons aren't any better (or worse) than anyone else's … just different.
- Focus on the positive and accept—even embrace—the negatives.
- Some "negatives" can be useful!
- People are a package deal … You don't get to pick and choose!

- Don't let minor differences become major conflicts with other people!
- If two people are totally compatible, one of them is useless!

He concluded, "*We are all fantastic individuals!*"

Shortly after that seminar Sarah (Tom's wife) was asked to list her greatest attributes and her weaknesses in order to sit on a leadership team at our church. Together we (Tom and Sarah) started listing her strongest qualities and how she could benefit our community. For example, we shared the following strengths:

- Steady. Through all of our lives' challenges she has remained consistent, patient, and faithful.
- Perceptive. She is quiet by nature, but her quiet nature allows her to take it all in. She watches, waits, and sees what others may be missing. She provides insight and discernment.
- Positive. When others tend to see what's wrong with a given situation, she tends to see the situation as an opportunity for growth. She give thanks and praise rather than dwelling on negativity.
- Gracious. She tries to see through others' flaws, shortcomings, and perceived "weaknesses," to see them as valuable, worthy, and significant. She values people based on who they are rather than what they accomplish.

She was also asked to describe her weaknesses. Based on what we had learned from Reinhardt's message a few days prior, we focused on the nuance of our words. Rather than saying that my wife is quiet and *therefore* doesn't speak up as much as she should, we suggested that being quiet helps her be more perceptive.

Every one of us has our strengths *and* those parts of us that make us unique. Some would call them weaknesses. But those perceived "weaknesses" or "oddities" or "shortcomings" are what make us who we are—and *we are all fantastic individuals!*

Obsession (Michael)

It's hard for me to put into words why I like the beach so much. Everything about it is renewing for me, almost like therapy.

—Amy Dykens

. . . .

Early each Father's Day morning is my favorite moment of the year. I enter our son Matthew's room to help him out of bed and get him dressed. And then it is my joy to say, "Matthew, guess where we're going today!"

He knows what's coming next. A huge smile breaks on his face. His steel-blue eyes twinkle and brighten. His hands start flapping. His legs begin twitching.

"To the beach!"

It is a wonderful Father's Day gift to myself.

His loud squeals pierce the room, alternately hurting my ears and filling me with enchantment. His entire body quivers, coiling with elation and anticipation. He claps his hands eagerly, unable to contain his absolute joy and delight. He can't focus on anything else now. He can neither eat nor drink. He's too excited; he is absolutely thrilled. Our annual weeklong trip to the beach is finally here. After a year of not-so-patiently waiting, it's time to go back again!

Matthew is obsessed with the beach—absolutely fixated on going there, on being there, on anticipating being there. He has other obsessions too. But the beach is his most constant and intense. He cannot speak, but he can clearly communicate, strongly and well, his desires about the beach. When we so often struggle to understand what he may want or need, there is no question about his feelings on that place. Because every day of the year he indicates that he wants to go to the beach. He points at the photos of him there that are all around our house. There are photos of past vacations—of him with his mother, of him with me, of him with his brothers, of him with his grandparents, and of him alone. In each one Matthew's joy is unmistakable. His joy is evident in his body language and in his broad, squinty-eyed grin. His excitement is unambiguous.

When it comes to the possibility of going to the beach, Matthew is eternally optimistic, perpetually hopeful, and infinitely expectant. He is relentless and unyielding.

His badgering is constant, and it can wear pretty thin some days. I'll be honest about that. His insistence can be frustrating, and it can fray our nerves.

He packs constantly. There are a lot of things he does not understand, a lot that he appears not to grasp. But, he absolutely knows what he believes he needs for the beach. He is obsessed about gathering tubes of sunscreen, swimsuits and T-shirts, Reese's Peanut Butter Cups, a towel, cups of pudding and a water bottle, and the Pull-Ups he wears because of his incontinence. If he can drag a beach umbrella up from the basement, he will insist on that being included too. He presents them to us and won't rest until as many of those necessities as possible are stuffed into a bag or backpack and set by the front door. Some days we pack those bags over and over again. Most days we are forever tripping over the bags and "necessities" by the door.

Matthew also wears a swimsuit and T-shirt twenty-four hours a day, 365 days a year. No matter how hot or cold it is, where he goes, or what the occasion he is, he wears a swimsuit. He wore one to both his older brothers' weddings, under his suit and tie, and to his high school graduation ceremony, under his gown. He wears one to church each Sunday, to his activities program each day, and to bed each night.

He has two dozen of them, in the bright, patterned colors he loves. There are extra swimsuits and T-shirts stowed in each of our cars and in the backpack he takes to his program each day. He has one packed in a bag that hangs on the back of the transport chair he uses when he is out in public.

The red swimsuits are his favorites. His Spiderman suits come next in the pecking order. Some of his swimsuits are threadbare and worn through, patched again and again to make them wearable as long as possible. When it's warm outside, a swimsuit and T-shirt will be all he wears wherever he goes. But when it's cold, his swimsuit and T-shirt are always on underneath another warmer shirt and a pair of long pants. When he had surgery and an eight-day hospital stay a few summers ago, he wore them instead of the standard-issue hospital gown.

Matthew is twenty-six years old and long past the age when wearing a swimsuit and T-shirt everywhere is considered cute or acceptable. But in his childlike innocence, in his autism and with his severe intellectual disabilities, they are simply part of who he is. His obsession is his joy. When he is on the beach, sitting on a low chair at the water's edge, he is calm and contented. Matthew rarely sits still—ever. He is always in motion, pulsing with frenetic energy, even in bed, even through the night.

But when he is at the beach—with the waves washing up to his feet, sometimes washing up over him, and occasionally crashing into him and knocking him and his chair over—he howls with laughter and glee. And he is tranquil, serene, and supremely contented—he is at peace. The packing has stopped. The obsession has paid off. He is finally at the beach.

And for at least this one week out of the year, Kathy and I can find tranquility, serenity, and contentment, and blessed peace on this journey we share together as well.

Stranded (Tom)

Not all of us can do great things. But we can do small things with great love.

—Mother Teresa

. . . .

My mind started wandering. I had been driving on I-79 North in our newly acquired used Jeep Cherokee with my pregnant wife through the mountains of West Virginia for nearly two hours. No radio. No cell phone service. No stoplights. No rest areas. No vehicles on the road other than ours. The only noise we heard was the slow drone of the wiper blades moving back and forth, reminding me of the metronome my fifth-grade piano instructor used to keep me on tempo. The slushy mix of snow, rain, and sleet started picking up, making it harder and harder to focus on the seemingly endless road before us.

It was the night before Christmas Eve, and we were making the long trek home to rural Pennsylvania. I was attending graduate school in Kentucky, and our winter break had finally arrived. My wife and I had to work earlier in the day, so we left later than we would have liked, forcing us to drive in darkness the entire trip home. We looked forward to the end of our eight-hour drive when we would be enjoying eggnog in front of a warm fireplace with our family.

Boom!

"Did you hear that?" I asked my wife.

"Yes. What happened?"

"I must have hit something," I said.

I pulled the vehicle off to the side of the road to check out the damage. I grabbed the flashlight from under my seat.

"We got a flat!" I yelled. "I'm going to put on the doughnut."

One by one I grabbed our Christmas presents from the trunk, placing them on the sloppy ground. I finally made it the bottom of the pile and grabbed the jack, our only source of hope on this wintry night.

"Great, it's broken! The car dealer sold us a vehicle with a broken jack! Now what?"

One by one I placed the saturated Christmas gifts back into the vehicle, replaying in my head how I could have made such a mistake. Why didn't I check everything before I bought the car? I returned to my seat to consider our next move. We took a moment to assess the situation and offer up a quick prayer.

We discussed our options:

1. We could see a house in the distance. Although it was hard to calculate how far away it was, we could walk and ring the doorbell.
2. I could walk to the next exit, which we figured was about fifteen miles away. Given my wife's pregnancy we decided it was too far for her to walk, so she could stay in the car until I returned.
3. We could wait in our car until another vehicle stopped to perform a modern-day Good Samaritan deed on our behalf. The car would be warm until the gas ran out. After that, we would stay dry until someone came by. (This option required a lot of hope; we hadn't seen another car on the road for nearly two hours).

Neither one of us liked options one or two, given that we were in rural West Virginia, so we decided on option three.

Neither of us expected to see another vehicle for several hours, so we decided to make the best of it. We could converse and enjoy one another's company. I reclined in my seat, and I shut off the wiper blades. As soon as I began to talk with my wife, I heard something that sounded like sirens. I looked in the rearview mirror and shouted as if we had just won the lottery. "A police car!"

The police officer pulled alongside our vehicle, introduced himself as Officer Anderson, and asked how he could be of service. I told him about the flat tire and that we didn't have a working jack or cell phone service.

Without hesitation, Officer Anderson hopped out of his vehicle, grabbed the jack from his car, plopped down on the soggy grass, and started changing the tire. He told us to stay inside our car where it was warm while he located a mechanic. The mechanic was forty-five miles away, and for the next hour and half, Officer Anderson followed behind our vehicle, even though it was out of his jurisdiction.

When we left our Jeep with the mechanic, Officer Anderson gave us a ride to a hotel. Before he left, I asked him for his police station address so I could send him a proper thank-you. I also asked a question that I had been mulling over since the moment he stopped to help us several hours before. "Why go out of your way like that?"

After a long pause, he looked me directly in the eyes and said, "I stopped to help you and your wife because someone stopped and helped me and my family when we were in need many years ago."

Officer Anderson's words have been reverberating in my heart and mind ever since that night. His words (and actions) have provided me with much hope in my life when we have faced difficult situations. His words have also been the driving force behind my mission in this life—to reach out and help those who are in need, those who are hurting, those who need compassion, and those who need someone to help carry their burdens.

The truth of the matter is that we all need an Officer Anderson from time to time. The bigger truth is that we can all be an Officer Anderson from time to time. Life gets challenging—a flat tire, a broken relationship, an unforeseen illness, a sudden job loss, or an unexpected bill to pay.

The day after Christmas I decided to contact the police station to properly thank Officer Anderson for his service. The police chief answered, and I started recounting the amazing act of kindness we had received from one of his officers. The police chief responded, "I'm very glad you received the help you needed the other night, but there isn't an Officer Anderson at our station."

To this day I'm not sure if there really is an Officer Anderson who roams the mountains of West Virginia on I-79 north. Perhaps he gave me a fictitious name so his good deed could be anonymous. Or perhaps he is simply an angel. One thing I know for certain, though; his amazing act of kindness has drastically changed the course of my life.

It's experiences such as this one, and so many others like it along life's journey, that teach me what it means to be empathetic to others who find themselves on difficult journeys too. People who feel stranded, lonely, surrounded by darkness, or lost all need an Officer Anderson in their lives just as we did that December 23 many years ago.

A Warm Embrace (Tom)

The best place in the world is in the arms of someone who will not only hold you at your best, but will pick you up and hug you tight at your weakest moment.

—Unknown

. . . .

The tears started streaming down her face. It had been a long, emotional few weeks for her, and the weight was taking its toll. Carrying twins for thirty-eight weeks could do that to any woman, but she had remained strong all the way to the finish! Finally, the twins had arrived!

Amid the elation surrounding their births, a new set of challenges had arisen. How would she be able to care for two newborns while her body tried to recover from the surgery? Three days in the hospital with sporadic sleep had caught up to her, and she had reached her breaking point. She wanted to go home and get her life back to the (whole new) normal of being the mother of four children under the age of five.

She had tried to hold it in but couldn't any longer; a steady flow of tears dampened the hospital pillow lying on her lap. In walked the surgeon who had performed her C-section. We expected him to simply give us the necessary information needed to care for herself and her two infants. But he didn't give information. He asked questions—personal questions— about her health.

"How are you really doing? You look upset. Are you disappointed you aren't able to leave today?"

More tears. Then the doctor said he would get her a box of tissues to catch her tears and dry her eyes. He walked away and returned with an unopened box of tissues, just for her, as he said he would.

The hospital was busy that day, but he didn't seem to care. In fact, he didn't pay any attention to anything other than her even though his phone kept ringing. He sat down next to her on the bed and simply let her cry.

After several minutes, she finally got a few words out.

"I'm just tired right now … really, really tired."

"I know," he said.

She stopped crying, and then he said, "I am very, very proud of you! We are all very, very proud of you! You are a wonderful mom." He went on, "You have done remarkably well. Better than almost every other mom who has ever carried twins before. This too shall pass. You are strong."

He then stood up and did something I have never seen any other doctor do—and I have spent a lot of my life in a doctor's office—he gave her a *hug*. A long, warm, tender hug. And she needed it.

There are times in all of our lives when we too need a long, warm, tender embrace. Maybe you are a mom and you are questioning your parenting abilities. You wonder whether or not you have what it takes to raise one, two, three, or four children. Maybe you recently went through a painful divorce and you are living with shame and guilt—even though you know it wasn't your fault. Maybe you recently lost a loved one and your life just isn't the same now and you are having a difficult time adjusting to the (whole new) normal.

It is moments like these when we all need a long, warm, tender embrace. We need to know we are loved. We need to be reminded that we have what it takes, that it wasn't our fault, and that time will bring healing. We need to be reminded that life will go on.

Michael and I hope that everyone can receive the peace, comfort, and consolation they need to help see them through. As Bob Dylan wrote in "Make You Feel My Love,"

> When the rain is blowing in your face
> and the whole world is on your case,
> I could offer you a warm embrace
> to make you feel my love.

Finding Joy in the Moment

While we try to teach our children all about life, our children teach us what life is all about.

—Angela Schwindt

. . . .

One summer night after work, as a treat, we took Tom's two oldest children to Hershey Park, a large amusement park near my home in Hershey, Pennsylvania. It was a hot midsummer night, and it seemed like a fun and refreshing thing to do.

As we were working at Tom's home throughout the day, Lillian, who was five at the time, and Luke, who was three, were super excited. Every five minutes one of them would ask when we would be leaving. They simply couldn't wait! We couldn't wait either. An evening at the park would be good for our souls.

We arrived at the park and were planning on riding just a few kiddie rides, rides Lillian and Luke had been talking about all afternoon. Hershey Park also has a nice water park area, but that wasn't part of our evening's plans. But the heat and humidity and the delighted laughter of so many kids—including Lillian and Luke—drew us in.

Without water shoes, towels, swimsuits, or sunscreen we were tentative at first, wondering if it was okay for them (and us) to get soaking wet. The kids were tentative at first too. In fact, Lillian said, "I don't know if I should go in without my bathing suit on." And Tom wondered what their mother would say if they came home soaking wet.

But the first pool of water we stepped in felt so refreshing on that hot and humid summer evening! There were fountains and waterfalls and sprays of water all around us. At first, we were careful to keep a safe distance from the sprays. But before long, the children began to lose their inhibitions. They tugged our hands and pushed us from behind, and before long we quickly lost our inhibitions too.

Soon enough, we all abandoned our concerns about staying dry; we gave in and got completely soaked. It felt so good, and it was so much fun. We surrendered and allowed joy and satisfaction to wash over us.

What a memorable night of simple fun! It was the kind of night that all of us need to have much more often than we do—a time when our inhibitions melt away and we can jump and play and laugh and give in to the child within us all.

There are trying times in our lives, sometimes long seasons in fact, when it seems as if our difficulties will never end. Maybe it's an illness, unemployment, a job we hate, a relationship gone bad, or grief over a devastating loss. Any one of those things can take us to dark and lonely places. In those times, joy can be difficult to find.

But joy is a gift that children can teach us to find again and again.

Childlike joy isn't dependent upon circumstances. It is easily evoked. Children are quick to abandon all inhibitions. They are quick to embrace simple delight. They are quick to pull us and push us from the burdens of our responsibilities and cares into the refreshing waters that wash away our seriousness and the gravity of our challenges.

As fathers, each one of our children has given us a gift of joy that we could so easily push aside—and sometimes we do. Joy is always needed, but sometimes we need to be reminded to look for it in the simple pleasures along the way.

There Comes a Time

There comes a time in all our lives when we must prepare for death. When we become old, get seriously ill, or are in great danger, we can't be preoccupied simply with the question of how to get better unless "getting better" means moving on to a life beyond our death. In our culture, which in so many ways is death oriented, we find little if any creative support for preparing ourselves for a good death. Most people presume that our only desire is to live longer on this earth. Still, dying, like giving birth, is a way to new life, and as Ecclesiastes says: "There is a season for everything: … a time for giving birth, a time for dying." We have to prepare ourselves for our death with the same care and attention as our parents prepared themselves for our births.

—Henri Nouwen

. . . .

He was in his final days. His family waited and surrounded him. They said their good-byes. They expressed their love. He was prepared. So were they—as much as it is possible.

He was loved. Dearly. While they didn't want him to go, they knew it was time. They'd given him permission. They'd said what they wanted to say. They'd surrounded him with love and devotion and tenderness.

And they were exhausted. They were on edge. Their wait felt excruciating at times.

Yet they surrounded him to make certain that his transition from this life was comfortable, peaceful, and enveloped in love. Their care and their faithfulness was beautiful.

They were able to laugh too. A soothing balm, their laughter came when it was needed most. Kidding each other as siblings do, they made fun of how one of them cooks, of how another was always cold, and of how another was always too hot. They laughed because that's what families do. They laughed and teased to reassure themselves that everything would be okay. They laughed to soothe their father too, hoping it would break through the veil of his ever-diminishing consciousness to remind him of their presence, of their love.

His death was a legacy, bonding them ever stronger, showing them the preciousness of life, and moving them to say what needed to be said, to put priorities where they needed to be, and to care for one another in their common grief and love.

It was a sacred privilege for us to share that intimate time with him and his family. We learned from them and feel grateful for their lessons of compassion and gratitude for the man who gave them life and love.

There is one thing that endures above everything else in this world, in this life, and that is love. It never ends. It is never taken away. It always lives on. It is love that, ultimately, consistently overcomes and conquers all the brokenness, all the distress, all the disappointment, all the disease, and all the death. When we feel as if we could break under the pain of regret, disillusionment, cynicism, discontentment, loss, and grief, we can be reminded that love is the one thing in life that lives on and has the healing power to revive and renew us, restore and refresh us.

When you're seventy-five years old, have been married for fifty-seven years, and leave behind a wife, a mother, three children, five grandchildren, two great-grandchildren, nieces and nephews, and great friends who love you dearly, it's hard to know just how those who love you will pick up the broken pieces and go on.

He is certainly, deeply, profoundly missed. But in love, his life will never end. It will go on.

Life is, ultimately, simply about love—love that is meant to show us how to find peace and joy and hope, even in the darkest, most difficult of our days. In dark seasons of our lives, we can, after a while, find light coming back and beginning to warm and brighten the world and our spirits. That light is love. The love we hold. The love we share. The love we feel for one another.

It is love that reminds us over and over again how we are lifted up and carried through. We are reminded that nothing—no evil, no loss, no pain, no disappointment, no regret, no death—can ultimately separate us from love. Even in sad and difficult times, we can celebrate and give thanks for that.

Life goes on because love goes on. Love never ends.

The Ache for Home (Tom)

The ache for home lives in all of us, the safe place where we can go as we are and not be questioned.

—Maya Angelou

. . . .

In seven years of marriage, we had moved seven times, and most of those moves weren't by our choosing. One of our landlords never fixed any issues at the house, which meant that many problems got increasingly worse over time. At another apartment we awoke at three in the morning our very first night because the cops had been called on our neighbor for domestic violence. His antics continued for many months, causing us many restless nights of sleep. Following that place, our next stop was my sister-in-law's attic. We had moved in with her family after I decided to leave my job suddenly and we didn't have a place to live. I left my position assuming I would be able to get another job shortly, but days turned into weeks, and weeks turned into months.

Author Maya Angelou once said, "The ache for home lives in all of us, the safe place where we can go and not be questioned." Her words couldn't be more true.

It wasn't just the moving that caused so much restlessness inside of us; it was the need to belong. Somewhere. Anywhere. There is nothing worse in this life than feeling as if you don't have a safe place to go, a safe place to be yourself, a safe place to simply *be*. But that is how we felt.

I wish I could say that was the last time we felt that way, but it wasn't. There was more moving, more uneasiness, and more discomfort in the next few years. After living in my sister-in-law's attic we moved to another apartment, where the neighbor downstairs complained repeatedly about having two small children living above him. In our next home, a double house, the neighbors in the other half commented disparagingly when they thought our children cried too much. Living in such close proximity with others made me feel anxious; I was fearful of their judgments about any noise our young kids made.

But we had each other. Through it all, our marriage stayed strong, our family shared love, and our faith carried us through.

In March 2013, we moved into our first home together. We couldn't be happier! We may not have gotten our dream home, but what we gained was something so much more important—that safe place where we could simply be who we had been created to be.

We look back on those experiences with gratitude. At times we felt like wanderers searching for the Promised Land. But each of those experiences has given us a passion to help those who feel as if they don't belong, as if they don't have a safe place in their own lives.

We all have an ache to belong somewhere, anywhere. We all need a home where we can be safe, where we can be understood, where we can be unconditionally loved. Sometimes the homes of our birth are those places—and that is good. We wish that for everyone, but we know that for many that isn't the case. And for them, home must be found somewhere else. But it is in this search that we can learn about ourselves, about family, about resilience, about faith, about love, about hope.

My prayer is that you will find home too—that you will find that place of comfort and security and safety, that place where you will not be questioned or rejected, that place where you can open your soul and know that, whatever happens, you will be taken in and enveloped by the warmth of love, grace, compassion, care, and acceptance.

Solitude

It's an interesting combination: Having a great fear of being alone, and having a desperate need for solitude and the solitary experience. That's always been a tug of war for me.

—Jodie Foster

. . . .

She pours out everything for us, sparing virtually nothing. Medical appointments. Visitors. Frustrations with neighbors. Her fatigue. Her fears. Anger at her situation. Her cat that pees on the floor. Doubts. Secrets. Dreams. The major developments and the daily minutia.

"You said I can tell you anything, right? You said not to hold it back. Well, here goes …"

And then it comes. She vents. She cries. She laughs. She shares. It's not always pretty. It's not always happy. It's both sacred and irreverent at the same time. Earthy and holy. She shares love and hate. Despair and hope. Every high and each new low.

She's lonely, and yet she longs for solitude. She rarely gets time alone, and yet she feels utterly alone most of the time. Her caregiving, for a parent who needs constant help and for her husband who is seriously ill and in and out of the hospital, drains her. She finds deep joy in her career, yet cannot work much because of her responsibilities at home. When she is able to work, she is often too drained to enjoy it.

There is chaos in her heart and soul, and she longs to find release from it.

Henri Nouwen has written:

> As soon as we are alone … inner chaos opens up in us. This chaos can be so disturbing and so confusing that we can hardly wait to get busy again. Entering a private room and shutting the door, therefore, does not mean that we immediately shut out all our inner doubts, anxieties, fears, bad memories, unresolved conflicts, angry feelings and impulsive desires. On the contrary, when we have removed our outer distraction, we often find that our inner distractions manifest themselves to us in full force. We often use the outer distractions to shield ourselves from the interior noises. This makes the discipline of solitude all the more important.

Solitude can bring out the best and the worst for us. In solitude, we can experience incredibly dark moments within our souls. We often fear being alone when those dark thoughts creep into our heads.

Yet we desperately need those moments, that solitude, to explore what is inside. And when we do, in those moments we can also find peace. In them, we can learn a lot about ourselves. Clarity. Direction. Our core values—the essence of who we are. We learn what is important to us. We can become centered and calm.

It is a tug of war for many of us. This search, this need, for solitude. Many of us fear it. But we shouldn't.

Ultimately, we need to foster compassion for ourselves, finding that safe place where we can explore the very depths of our souls. Confronting the demons, facing the fears, and walking through the inner darkness can ultimately be healing for us. The demons and fears come to light and begin to be less frightening. They can help us find hope in our circumstances, especially the hardest ones.

An Indomitable Will

Strength does not come from physical capacity. It comes from an indomitable will.

—Mahatma Gandhi

. . . .

Since it started, it hasn't stopped.
The ground rumbles. A deafening roar. Foundations shake. Buildings fall. People die.

In Christchurch, New Zealand, it has been going on since February 2011. Two and a half years of destruction, setting everyone on edge when we talked with them about it. It's trauma—physical, emotional, and spiritual—that will not end.

When we spoke with them on Skype that day, we heard their stories, and we were moved. They eloquently shared what it's been like. They spoke of the close friends they've lost, more than thirty-five of them. They shared the terror they felt when the first quake hit and the constant aftershocks. They talked about the calls in the middle of the night from those needing to share their fear and horror.

They told us about their city and the tens of thousands of people who have fled since it all began. They grieve for the lives that were lost. They remember the landmarks no longer there. They live in a city that is very different now, one in which the ground can suddenly open up and swallow them. They fear driving at night because they never know if the road will disappear in an instant and devour the car. They keep their children and grandchildren close by; they never know when another quake will strike. Loss is so much a part of daily life now. Homes. Jobs. Security. Peace. Loved ones. All have disappeared much too often and much too quickly in these last few years.

Our friends are suffering. The losses and the traumas have simply piled up and continue. We can hear it in their voices. We can see it in their eyes. We can read it in their words when they write to us. These last couple of years have been a time of deep hurt and profound fear. Survivor's guilt. Constant uncertainty. Waiting for the next one. It takes its toll.

Yet ...

They persevere. They don't give up. They find ways to laugh and celebrate. They rely on their faith in goodness and grace that exists beyond themselves. They hold those they love closer. They love ever stronger, ever more. They embrace the life they have, knowing it is fragile, precious, and miraculous.

And they listen.

They listen to the cries of their friends, opening themselves to the mournful expressions of their hearts. They support. They encourage. They pray. They hold hands. They wipe tears. They touch souls with a message of compassion and comfort.

They have an indomitable will, a strength that lifts them up and soothes the troubled spirits all around.

We are privileged to know them and honored to call them our friends.

My Birds

Find a place inside where there's joy, and the joy will burn
out the pain.

—Joseph Campbell

• •

"**I**t's complicated," she exclaims many times as we talk. "It's
complicated, crazy, and sometimes I just can't believe it's happening
to me."

She lays it out:

The surgery following an accident. The long hospital recovery. The rehab that
went on longer. The mental fog caused by the pills and pain relievers. The
four feet of snow that dumped on her home right after she returned from the
hospital, isolating her. The sadness and hurt that came when no one called to
see how she and her husband, for whom she is a caregiver, were doing. The
hurricane that destroyed much of her roof and flooded her basement later that
year. The two-year insurance red tape and bureaucracy battle that is still going
on. The roof that is still not fixed two years later. The fault line that her home
is on and the small earthquake that followed, shaking both her belongings
and her spirit. The severe pain that never goes away. The alienation from her
family members whom she believes callously ignore her struggles and offer
neither support nor help. Her husband's depression and seclusion.

She indicates that's not all of it.

Yes, it is complicated. Deeply so.

Her loneliness is deeply felt. Her husband won't talk. Her family doesn't seem to want to hear it. Her friends have quickly faded away.

She simply needs to talk, to share it, to try to give voice to the disappointments, doubts, and dysfunctions of the system and those around her. She's trying, desperately, to sort it out and to find a way to keep going in spite of it. It's so complicated that it immobilizes her. Her life has lost its hope. Her spirit has lost its faith.

We asked her, "What in your life is able to bring you joy? Is there anything right now that inspires you? Anything that gives meaning to your life?"

Her response surprised us: "My birds."

"Your birds?"

"I take in rescue birds. At one time I had twenty-seven of them at my home. Macaws to parakeets. I just love them. Caring for them. Feeding them. Nursing them back to strength and health. They are my joy."

There it was—her joy. Those birds filled her with life, with meaning, with purpose. Yet the sad—and tragic—thing was, when she got sick, there were those who wanted to take her birds away.

And they did.

Her joy. Without it her life held little meaning. If others would have taken the time and been intentional about listening to her, really listening and getting to know her, maybe they would have come to understand that. All of us have something in our lives than can bring us meaning and that can fill us with purpose. It's not for anyone else to discount that. In our listening we can help draw that out for each other. That's one very important thing we can do for one another. It may have been a small thing, but her birds were something. In losing them her world fell apart. She needed those birds to help give her life.

To Celebrate Those Moments (Tom)

You cry and scream and you stomp your feet and you shout. You say, "You know what? I'm giving up, I don't care." And then you go to bed and you wake up and it's a brand new day, and you pick yourself back up again.

—Nicole Scherzinger

. . . .

I took a long walk around my neighborhood one Sunday morning. It was a nearly perfect fall day. The sky was bright and blue. The sun illuminated the quickly changing leaves and made their red, orange, and gold colors shine beautifully. I loved it.

Everything in my world was great during that walk. I didn't want it to end.

After my walk I read the Sunday paper. My habit when I read the paper was to ease into the news by turning to the comics section first. I savored those moments too, simply because they provided a more gentle start to the day. But within minutes that quickly changed as I viewed the headlines:

"Man Shot in Head"

"Three Dead in Fire"

"Kenya Mall Becomes War Zone ..."

"Roaring Waters Leave Deep Scars in Colorado"

And I already longed for those earlier moments of respite when I walked around the neighborhood and laughed at the comics. In those moments life was aligned the way it was meant to be.

It's those moments that keep me going.

The night before was another painful one, an especially painful one physically. My fibromyalgia was flaring up ... again. Before I fell asleep, I desperately wanted the day to end, for sleep—and relief—to come, at least for a few hours. I just wanted the day to be over. I longed for a new day, to start all over again.

But in my dark hours of agony and desperation, I have learned something vital. I have learned to celebrate those moments, fleeting as they so often are, when everything is in alignment.

When I'm not in pain or anguish.

When the sun is shining brightly.

When the leaves begin to turn brilliantly colorful.

When I can ease into the day.

When no bad news has yet taken the solace away.

I appreciate the moments so much more because I know they can be fleeting. I savor their goodness because of the blessed hope and comfort they bring.

The Need to Please
(Michael)

When I was hidden, everybody was paying for it. Even
if they didn't know it. Everybody was being robbed
of the best of who I was. Even when I was on my
game, I couldn't give you the real stuff God put inside
me to give away. People wanted to love me, but they
couldn't. People wanted me to love them, but I couldn't.
Everybody lost ... The goal is not just for someone's
exposure, but their freedom—so everyone gets the best
of you.

—John Lynch, Bruce McNicol, and Bill Thrall, *Bo's Cafe*

. . . .

I sat there horrified as he did it. At lunch for a meeting, my supervisor
berated the young server for an offense only he seemed to see. As she
stood there wilting under his ire, I sat there wanting to melt too.

Mute. Not knowing what to do. In my opinion she didn't do anything
wrong. But she did in my boss's eyes, and he felt the need to let her know.
Harshly. Publically.

"And the gratuity will reflect it too!" was his parting shot before he dismissed her and she slunk away.

I'd seen him do it before. To coworkers, a lot. To me, once or twice. I knew how it felt. I felt bad for her, but I stared down at the table, wishing I was anywhere but there. And I sat there, silent.

The second we got in the car on the way back to the office he spoke up. "I won't apologize for what I just did."

He knew that it had bothered me. It would have bothered anyone who witnessed it. But he didn't care.

"I expect better service than what she gave, and she needed to know that. You should expect it to. I don't apologize for what I said."

I struggled to respond, tempering what I really wanted to say. Out came some innocuous response; I said virtually nothing. I knew that to challenge him only created more tension, more indignation on his part. So I avoided it. And I felt lousy about it.

He was rude. He was mean. He was unreasonable. He was wrong. But since he was my boss, I voiced none of those beliefs. And I suffered in my silence, along with a young server who was certainly suffering too.

I'm haunted by moments such as those—moments when I didn't speak up to defend someone, moments when people stepped over reasonable lines, moments when I didn't want to displease someone who had some power over me.

Why is it so hard at times to stand up for what I think is right or against what I think is terribly wrong?

Why is the pull to be liked, to please others, so strong at times that I would rather deny part of myself and my principles and live in silence?

What causes that fear? What keeps me shut in? What stops me from allowing the courage of my convictions to come out?

I'm a work in progress, continuously growing. Continuously trying to let the best of me be seen. Continuously looking for ways to begin the conversations that give permission for the best of all of us to be revealed.

Out of the Fires

Things get bad for all of us, almost continually, and what
we do under the constant stress reveals who/what we are.

—Charles Bukowski

. . . .

A friend from California spoke of terrible wildfires that raged several
years ago very near his home, leaving a massive swath of destruction
behind them. The landscape was left eerily barren, much like the surface
of the moon.

But our friend mentioned something else, something he noticed after
those fires that he had never really noticed much before. Out of the ashes
there had sprouted an abundance of flowers. Brilliant reds and purples,
magnificent colors, bright and intense, had begun to bloom, as if they'd
never seemed to bloom before. Out of seeming death had come life. Out of
a bleak landscape had come renewal—of a most spectacular kind. The fires
in their destructive fury may have burned away much of what had been
growing on the land, but the fires couldn't destroy what lay beneath the
surface there. In fact, the fires created the conditions for these magnificent
flowers, with their incredible colors, to come to life so brightly.

Our friend was stunned by what he saw, by what he had never noticed
before—before the cancer that had entered his life, before the fires, before
the threat all around him. But after his journey with disease and his
experience from the fires he now noticed. He came through the fires and

was safe. He came through the fires, and his property and life were not destroyed. He came through those fires, as well as the threatening fires of cancer, and now he sees life in a different, a much more appreciative, way.

"I never paid attention before," he said. "But now I do. I'm more alive now than I was before. Things are just clicking with me. I see beyond myself now, beyond the petty challenges of life. Now I see the bigger picture."

Once you've been through any fire—disease, loss, brokenness, life-altering challenges—you really can notice things that you never noticed before.

A guide who Tom heard at Yellowstone National Park once said this about wildfires: "Most people think of wildfires as this horrible thing. But in fact, Yellowstone, and many other forests, *need* wildfires to help reproduce and experience growth. Nature has a way of making it through some of the most horrible situations."

He described certain pinecones that have a special coating enabling them to withstand wildfires. These pinecones are dropped after the fires, which initiates the reproduction process. The fires actually cause them to be stronger and more fruitful.

Humans can possess that ability too.

Think about it. What do you notice because of the fires in your life? What is more brilliant to you? More clear? More understandable? What has been enhanced?

Fires can temper us. The fires—the challenges, the intensity, the heat that comes with profound vulnerability—can help us to view our lives and the world around us in a brand-new, better way. Ultimately, we hope that new way can truly bring all of us a sense of wonder, beauty, and peace as we've never known before.

A Stranger, Reaching Out (Michael)

To walk alone is possible, but the good walker knows that the great trip is life and it requires companions.

—Dom Helder Camara

. . . .

Often, we look for miracles to be big, dramatic events—occurrences that suddenly alter our lives in ways we never expect. Certainly, they can and do come that way. But those kinds of miracles are usually rare. Spectacular and breathtaking, yes. But definitely rare.

More frequently, though, I see miracles occurring every day, quietly and subtly but just as unexpectedly and just as profoundly. These miracles—of goodness and grace—remind us that we are not alone, encouraging us in our struggles, giving us the strength to keep going even when the path ahead is littered with great challenge and obstacles that threaten to defeat us ...

The day begged for us to be outside. It was the first Saturday in March, and a record high temperature for the day was being set. The bleakness of late winter was shattered by spring's sudden burst of life. People were out everywhere, throwing off overcoats and knit hats, donning shorts and flip-flops. Even if it was temporary, it felt wonderful to grasp the weather's respite, to enjoy it as long as it would last, even if only for a day.

It was a perfect afternoon for a long walk on a wooded bike trail I had discovered a year before. I looked forward to a couple of hours of exercise and refreshment for my soul, taking Matthew with me. I was excited to be out without having to steel myself, to brace from the cold.

The trail was full of people, everyone smiling, greeting one another, taking pleasure in the sweet anticipation of spring.

At one point, a young boy rode his bike toward us, his father riding closely behind. The dad and I exchanged hellos as they passed, and we continued on our way.

A little while later, the father and his son passed us again, this time coming from behind. The dad slowed and turned to me. He looked intently at Matthew and asked, "Do you mind if I talk with you for a moment?"

"No, not all," I replied.

He introduced himself and his son. I introduced Matthew and myself.

"Do you mind if I ask about Matthew's condition?"

"Certainly not. Matthew has severe intellectual disabilities and autism."

"How old are you, Matthew?"

Since Matthew couldn't, I replied for him. "Matthew's twenty-one. But he can't talk."

Then he asked me something that took me very much by surprise, something no stranger had ever asked me out of the blue like that before: "Do you mind if we pray for him?"

"No, I don't," I said. I was touched by his concern, his unashamed show of compassion.

He asked his son to put his hand on Matthew, and he did the same. He began to pray, "Lord, I just ask that you—"

Matthew, who because of his autism dislikes being touched, shook off both of their hands, interrupting the prayer. But the man resumed and soon concluded with "—show them your healing and your love. Amen."

All the while, an incredible sense of peace and calm washed over me. Here was a stranger, reaching out to us in empathy because he recognized the challenges I had with Matthew. I recognized this as a very special moment, a unique moment, bonding us. But I had no idea how much we shared until we kept talking after the prayer.

I thanked him for the prayer. As we spoke, I learned that he was a music teacher. I told him that my full-time work (at that time) was with people living with cancer—counseling, leading support groups, writing, directing programs to encourage them. We learned that we each had three sons; his older two were actually riding on the path ahead of him. He shared with me that his youngest son also had a developmental disability, a problem with reading for which he was receiving special help. He said that twenty-five years earlier he had worked in a group home for people like Matthew. I realized that he really could empathize in some way with our challenges.

I told him that my wife, Kathy, had been diagnosed with breast cancer four and a half years earlier, that we were so grateful that it was discovered early and that she was now doing well. I explained that I had taken Matthew out for the afternoon to give Kathy a break, because I knew at times the weight of Matthew's care could be incredibly heavy and that each of us needed periodic breaks.

His next comment was thoroughly unexpected. He said that his wife also had breast cancer, that she was diagnosed around the same time as Kathy. But instead of being cancer-free, she was in stage IV, at the end stage of her journey. He and his sons were out riding also just to take a break, to find a little respite, while a friend stayed home to care for her.

I struggled with a response. He was obviously in pain. His challenges were heavy beyond belief. I could only imagine how difficult it was for him. I wondered how to encourage him.

Yet there he was, providing me with a moment of grace, reminding me that even a stranger could express profound concern and care. We were connecting on deep and yet common ground.

Three sons. Special needs. Breast cancer. Faith in something beyond ourselves.

"I know this must be so hard," I responded, quietly. "I'm so glad you can take this small break. I know you need it."

His mind suddenly seemed to be transported to another place. And then: "I need to be going, to catch up with my other sons."

I told him I'd pray for him too. They rode away. I stood watching them leave, trying to process what had just taken place.

In the magnificent warmth of that Saturday afternoon, I reflected on the fact that I had just encountered an angel. He was an angel of mercy and understanding, coming to me when I least expected it. I hoped he felt that he had encountered an angel too. We were like mirrors for one another, reflecting so much of our circumstances and ourselves in each other's eyes. Each of us was praying for the other's needs, for the brokenness to be healed, for the pain to be soothed, for the burdens to be lifted.

A small miracle. An everyday encounter. Someone showed his interest, showed that he cared. These miracles can—and do—happen all the time. These miracles—of goodness and grace—remind us that we are not alone. They encourage us in our struggles. They give us the strength to keep going even when the path ahead is littered with great challenge and obstacles that threaten to defeat us.

But they don't, because these miracles are real. Every day.

Why Is Life So Incredibly Hard?

To live is to suffer, to survive is to find some meaning in the suffering.

—Friedrich Nietzsche

. . . .

She wanted us to write her story. She had the title: "Thought of a new title for the book: *It Happened Twice.*" She asked us virtually every time we spoke, weekly, if we'd made progress on it and how it was coming along.

She would always say she wanted it to be written to express the often horrific nature of cancer, both for those living with it and, in her case, those caring for someone with it.

She had first called Michael four years before, to receive support as her husband was dying with cancer. She called every other week and wrote messages in between. She was distraught, frightened, lonely, and in agony over what was happening. The day he died she called, sobbing, barely able to talk. She continued to call and write hundreds of times after that as she processed her despair and her grief. She hated the thought, the reality, that she was a widow, at a much-too-young age. She didn't know how she would cope.

But one day, after a few years, she met a man. As she shared about him, he sounded wonderful. He was what she needed. No longer did she sob through each call. No longer were there confessions of despair. She was talking about starting over again. She was laughing. She was falling in love.

He asked her to marry him. She was thrilled. She said yes.

She also said she was scared. Her greatest fear, after losing a husband at a young age, fifty-one, was that it could happen again.

Two months after their wedding, she called again. She was at work, and she was hysterical. Unintelligible. A coworker had to take the phone and speak for her.

Her new husband, of just two months, the man who was helping her find new life again, had just been diagnosed with the same cancer that had ended her first husband's life.

In subsequent phone calls she would ask, over and over, "How can this happen to me again?"

It was then that we both began talking with her and her husband over the phone, nearly every week. She wrote often on the days in between. For a year we listened, we encouraged, we comforted, and we did our best simply to love them through a painful, devastating situation.

And then the call came.

They committed suicide, together.

After we learned the news, Michael questioned, "Did we do enough? Did we say enough? Did we share enough? Did we respond appropriately enough?"

Tom reflected, "For four years you listened to her. You comforted her and encouraged her. For the last year both of us listened together to them every week. We really tried our best to help them know they were not alone. We affirmed them when they sought other professionals to help them process what they were going through. I not sure what else we could have done."

We sought counsel from another pastor, who has provided pastoral support to thousands of people throughout his career. He reminded us that sometimes there was nothing more anyone else could do. This insight of his illuminated a stark truth: "Sometimes life is just too incredibly hard."

For her, especially, it truly was, as she attested to in the weeks before they'd simply had enough.

> October 10
> Yesterday the doctor actually said, "I've never heard of anything like you're going through, I've never even read about anything like this ..."
>
> It doesn't help when people say that, in fact in many ways it makes me feel worse, although I know it's not said with that intent. I happened to mention "when he is cured" and the doctor corrected me saying, "remember there is no cure." I just looked at him and said, "But I'm still allowed to hope for that miracle." Sometimes I just want to scream from the roof tops, please, don't take my hope away. It's all I've got left. And why wouldn't I see it that way? It's only destroyed my life twice, taken my happiness, destroyed my hopes and dreams, turned my life into two separate living nightmares. Who wants to share their life with that kind of a monster?
>
> I'm tired of seeing people gasp in disbelief. I'm tired of hearing them say they've never heard, or even read, of such a thing. I'm tired of hearing them say that I must be like one in five billion, if there's anyone else at all. I'm just tired.
>
> October 14
> Another night with that breathing sound. Didn't fall asleep until after 4:30 a.m. That same horrible sound, that same

dreadful noise. I thought I'd never hear that noise again. Same chest pains. He can barely stay awake for more than 10 minutes. Same fear, is he really getting enough oxygen when he's sleeping and breathing like this????

Arguing with the doctors. The cursed radiation. The cursed cyber knife. Cancer. Is this how it always goes??

Same nightmare, same horror all over again.

We heard that same frustration over and over and over again, usually through tears of anger and anguish. In almost every email. In almost every phone call she would ask, "Have you ever heard of this happening to someone more than once? Does this ever happen to anyone else?"

In what would become the last two months of her life her anguish and anger came through in her emails very clearly:

October 16
I finally figured something out … When I met him, he brought love and laughter back into my life, had so much in common too. When we got married, I felt so protected, safe and secure again.

With the cancer diagnosis, those last three things disappeared in a flash. Now I don't know how to fix it, and I find it hard to move forward without it … I no longer feel protected, safe or secure with him. How do you live that way in a marriage, when that part is gone forever?

October 23
… I'm very, very SCARED. Now he sleeps most of the day, falls asleep early at night. I go for long walks alone on the beach. I eat alone most of the time. A month ago we where at his nephews wedding, danced the night away, everyone said how great he looked. Two weeks ago we got great news, then that Friday his neck blew up like a

bullfrog. He doesn't look good, he doesn't feel good … déjà vu.

What am I going to do? Can't handle this … you know my fear. We came here to help him live. I'm terrified that I'm watching him die instead.

October 26
I'm tired, I've carried the ball for eight months now. Life is different now, it ALWAYS will be. But he still fights it and complains about it constantly. I can't take it anymore. He almost died … I needed this like I needed a giant hole in my head. So yes, at the moment, I'm really furious!!!!!

October 29
I am also tired, very tired. I have given up my job, my health benefits, and myself to be a caregiver and manage his care. It has been eight months and I want to move forward with my life, with our lives. I am tired of being in limbo, with no idea of where we're going. All of my life I have done as "others" wanted. Honestly, I hate to admit it, but I'm growing very resentful. I don't want to leave or lose him. But given our situation, I feel it's time "to do it my way."

November 10
Love is such a deep emotion, so hard to understand the power of it. When your heart is broken, or you're hurt or scared, love makes it soooo much harder. If I didn't love him this would hurt so much less, not be nearly as hard or as frightening. Yesterday we had a huge argument, a real blowup. I told him not to buy me an anniversary card, or a gift. I told him there is no anniversary card that could celebrate "this," what we've had for our first year of marriage. I find myself dreading the date, and last year this time I was so filled with happiness, hope,

anticipation, and love. I felt the love becoming anger, by the time we went to bed, I felt the anger becoming hate. Then I woke up beside him this morning and realized all over again that I love him so much, that this would all be simpler and easier in many ways if I didn't. That it's the love that makes it all hurt so deeply, makes me so anxious and afraid. Waiting and hoping again that our lives will go back to some type of "normal," that we will still "have" a life together. Or is it all gone? Will it always be about cancer? Will I live every day in fear?

November 16

I don't share this with him (how could I), but I often feel like Job in the Bible, with an added twist. I lost everything after my first husband died. My entire world crumbled before my very eyes. I would often think about the story of Job. Then I met him, and everything's changed. I loved his parents, his family, some of his friends. My life became so full again. And now I see it crumbling again. I thought in the story of Job, when God gave him everything back in additional measure, it was for keeps. Now I can already feel the divide. It will almost be like a divorce, his friends are his friends. I've even noticed a distinct distancing with my own friends. They've all "been there done this before" with me. They don't want to (can't really) do it again, it's too hard for them. They were all elated for me a year ago this time. I had made it out of the depths of despair, into a new life, only to see it crumble so quickly, right back to exactly where I was. I think in some ways it's almost a "reflex" type of reaction. So scary to others that this could actually happen to me twice, that they pull away, because what if this happens to them? Too painful to have watched it once, and then watch it again. My own mother (who we know is not the most stable example), told me, "I helped you pick up the pieces before, I'm happy with my life now, so don't expect me to do it again." Imagine how many tears I shed after that one!

I feel lost, boxed in with no door to exit. There will be no happy ending here. It hurts, it hurts everyday … Living with constant emotional pain and stress is agony, no doubt about it. It's exactly the same as living with constant physical pain. Our society just doesn't get that.

I'm hurting, and I can't seem to make it stop. I'm getting tired … I'm in a marriage where I'm lonely and alone a lot. A year ago I married my best friend, my soul mate, the man who brought so much joy and happiness into my life. And here it is, gone again so quickly. Replaced with so much sadness and fear.

We thought we had more time to write her story. We thought there was much more of her story yet to unfold. We prayed that it would end happily. She said she wanted that too. But it simply wasn't to be.

It was just a few days before Christmas when we received a call from the state police. Our minds immediately went to a dark place—someone had died. We were right, sadly.

It was her—and her husband. They took their own lives. The officer relayed the news, and we were stunned. The officer said, "You were at the top of a list that they left, for people to be notified. Did you know them? How did you know them? What was your relationship?"

Life for her was just too incredibly hard, as she would often cry. In the end she decided that she had enough and that there was no other way out of the pain but to leave this life. We have no idea when she came to that conclusion or when her husband joined her in that decision. Despite our encouragement, despite our best efforts to help her and her husband find light in their darkness, in the end they just could not find it. It saddened us deeply. It's a sadness that lingers over a year later. We so desperately wanted them—as we do everyone—to find a way out of despair or doubt or pain. But we also have come to believe that sometimes for some people life is just too hard, just too dark, just too anguished. Sometimes, some people just can't find another way beyond the intense ache of despondency and hopelessness. But we wish they could.

Sometimes our hearts simply have to ache for them, for those who cannot find their peace.

The way through the darkness, the pain, the sorrow, and the brokenness is to share it with others who will enter into the darkness with you. That's what we tried to do for her. But in the end it's up to each of us to receive it.

She just wasn't able to receive it, though. We know that she tried; she really did. But in the end, she wasn't able to find the peace she needed in this life. An earlier message conveyed her struggle and her conflict:

> August 12
> You know I've basically given up on God and that whole thing. But please, please, if both of you could pray, it would be greatly appreciated. There is no peace. There is no God. I would ask you to pray. But I know from experience that doesn't help. That doesn't work.
>
> God will always make a way?
>
> I have simply come to the conclusion that if there is a God, he has no control over what happens here, and if he truly is a loving God, then he would understand that no one could possibly stay sane and intact with so much pain, for such a prolonged period of time.

It was just too hard. There are times such as these when we just don't know why life has to be like this. All our theological training hasn't helped us to answer these questions with certainty and with ease. There just aren't neatly packaged responses when life is this hard. Platitudes don't help. In fact, they make it worse. When someone is hurting this much, when life continues to bring heartache, horror, and fear, there is often nothing that any of us can say or do to "fix" what is so horribly wrong.

So all we can do is offer our presence and our hearts, allowing the pain to have companions of grace, compassion, and love—the only, and best, gifts we know to give.

A Wonderful World? (Michael)

The tree which moves some to tears of joy is in the eyes of others only a green thing which stands in their way.

—William Blake

. . . .

I do not cry easily.

But without warning, and with sudden explosiveness, tears poured out one morning. It was a surprising release of emotion—cathartic and intense.

I was reading a magazine article about another family's profound challenges with two sons who were born with severe developmental disabilities. Many of their experiences were similar to ours. Their fears and worries for the future were much like ours. The husband and wife ordered their daily lives around their sons' unique and demanding needs. So did we. Their decision to compromise their careers to raise their sons with dignity and love was another similarity we shared.

But what caused my emotional eruption was reading about the father's own sudden and unexpected shedding of tears while at a pub with his brother and his buddies. According to the brother, the father's tears flowed freely upon hearing the song "What a Wonderful World," the Louis Armstrong classic.

I hear babies cry ... I watch them grow.
They'll learn much more ... than I'll ever know.
And I think to myself ... what a wonderful world.
Yes, I think to myself ... what a wonderful world.

I could resonate strongly with the emotions of that father. The words of that song are bittersweet. Life with a child who has disabilities is bittersweet.

"I hear babies cry ... I watch them grow."

Our son rarely cried. He didn't ... still doesn't ... have that emotional ability. He never grew like his brothers. Today, at age twenty-six, he's very short and slight.

"They'll learn much more ... than I'll ever know."

He hasn't learned much more than I'll ever know. In fact, he seems permanently stuck in a two-year-old's world. He doesn't talk. He still wears diapers. He can't feed himself without creating a huge mess. He can't dress himself.

But he can undress and will do so at the most inappropriate times. In fact, he wears a shirt buttoned to the neck and a necktie every day, no matter where he's going or what he's doing, because he doesn't know how to undo them, and so he stays dressed.

He pulls his mother's hair when he wants her attention. He hits me, because my hair's too short to pull, when he wants mine.

In short, he's a handful. He rarely stops moving, even in his sleep. He throws whatever he can and enjoys the sound of something shattering on the floor—and our startled reactions to it. If he doesn't get his way immediately and just as he wants it, he'll bang his head on the living room picture window or the family room glass door. His head has gone through a few windows that way, so he knows it will get a reaction. The floors are sticky because of the things he spills. The walls are streaked with the residue of food he's thrown. All our furniture is banged up, scratched, and stained.

His loud bellowing interrupts our conversations. His relentless badgering for us to do whatever he wants is relentless. He is obsessed with the beach. He packs bathing suits, towels, and sunscreen all day long when he's home—every day of the year. He'll throw himself to the floor of the grocery store if we don't pick up packages of hot dogs or bottles of soda or—for some reason—multiple packs of paper napkins.

In church, he claps repeatedly, disrupting the service, and squawks incessantly if he doesn't like the music. He demands attention and knows how to get a reaction by the inappropriate and often dangerous and destructive things he does.

Yes, "What a Wonderful World" is a bittersweet song for me. Caring for our son and meeting his needs is a relentless and draining job. There is so little about him that makes our lives easy. There is so little that is uncomplicated. We need to plan well and think through details. Little happens spontaneously. I've had to alter my professional life considerably because of him. It's hard to maintain and sustain friendships because of the limitations his care imposes. Interests outside of work and home are nearly impossible for us. Life is harder for us because of him.

"And I think to myself … what a wonderful world."

And yet in spite of all that and the stressful and challenging days we have with our son, I can declare that it is still a wonderful world. In spite of our son's limitations, those he inherited at birth and those his realities inherently placed on us, there is still so much more that is good.

Those moments when his steel-blue and vibrant eyes actually focus on mine—rare for a person with autism—melt my heart. His smile, with its wildly crooked teeth and food often caked around his mouth, melts my will and warms my spirit. His laugh, raucous and uninhibited, generously employed and full-throated, melts any anger and frustration he may have caused moments before.

And when he leans in to allow me to hug him or kiss him? That alone melts into my soul and leaves me in complete and utter love.

I know that so much of what he does (and so much of what he cannot and does not do) is out of his control. I know that his developmental disabilities, severe and multiple, bring limitations to him and to us. But those limitations have truly shown me what it means to love unconditionally. To love regardless. To love in spite of. To love even when I am changing adult diapers or washing layers of fingerprints and mouth prints off the windows several times a week.

Those limitations have shown me how to love unconditionally, even when I say "I love you" and never hear it back.

I never asked for this world. I never would have wished for it the way it is. But it is our world, and as hard as it so often is, I still think to myself, *It's a wonderful world.*

And that can easily make me cry ..., with complete and utter joy.

Mentors

Mentor: Someone whose hindsight can become your foresight.

—Unknown

· ·

Tom

I was a college communications major. Between my sophomore and junior years, I took an internship at a large public relations firm on Wall Street, in New York City. For three weeks I worked in what felt to me like a very toxic environment. With each passing day, it got harder and harder for me to go to work. I felt like the lead character in the movie *Office Space* who declares, "Every day I go to work is the worst day of my life; every day is worse than the day before."

After grinding it out each day, I felt desperately that something needed to change. I realized that public relations was not the field for me. One afternoon, at the end of a long, discouraging day, my supervisor—a woman in her fifties who had worked at the firm for decades—and I walked to the ferry that would take us to New Jersey where we both lived. As we were walking, she sensed that something was wrong. I remember she turned to me, looked me directly in the eyes, and said, "Why are you doing this? There's more that you can do with your life. And you need to do it."

I started to cry. Through my tears I responded, "Why do *you* stay here?" I had sensed that she was not content in her job either.

"I can't leave. I've worked here too long. I need the money, and I don't know what else I could do with my life at this age. But you're still young, and you can do it differently. Follow your dreams. Don't get stuck doing something that you hate, something that is only a dream that someone else has for you."

I had only known her for three weeks, and I have not seen her since. But in that moment, she was a vital mentor to me. Even though our time working together was brief and fleeting, she served a significant role in my life. Her wisdom and experience gave me permission to acknowledge the truth about who I am and the truth about who I need to be.

Her words encouraged me to reflect upon and reconsider my path, the course for my life. I resigned my position that week and recalibrated my future. I am so grateful for her insights, for her encouragement to take a risk, for her support and understanding. The vulnerability that she showed in acknowledging her own discontentment enabled me to avoid a discontented path of my own. I am forever grateful for her for that.

Michael

I had a college internship too. Between my junior and senior years of school, I worked in the office of a Pennsylvania state senator, the only serving female senator in the state at that time.

The senator already had a long and esteemed career in public service when I went to work for her. Unlike Tom, I absolutely loved my internship. I was majoring in government and public service, and I felt a calling to serve so that I could help provide a better quality of life for others.

I respected the senator highly. I appreciated the rest of her staff. Each of them treated me with dignity and were very generous to me that summer. It was a dream job for a college kid; a refreshing sense of duty, honor, integrity, compassion, and respect for the common good were modeled for me. As I observed how the senator and her staff approached their responsibilities, I saw people who were forthright examples of what public service and politics were meant to be at their best. I will always be tremendously grateful for that internship and for the mentors who shepherded me through it. Their example of service, more than thirty years ago, is alive and strong in me today.

Ultimately, I left my career in government and public service. I realized that my best gifts required me to serve others in a different way. I learned, starting with my internship, that I was called to serve by counseling, writing, teaching, and affirming others to be exactly who they were created to be; I was called to mentor others. These powerful mentors of my senate internship showed me how to use my strongest gifts for the common good.

The best mentors teach us more than we realize at the time. But in time, their lessons grow and equip us in ways we never expected. Their lessons will take us places and remain with us in those places for the rest of our lives.

Tom and I believe that everyone can be a mentor. Everyone has something to offer, something to teach the world. We believe that by seeing everyone as having inherent value and sacred worth, we can learn from one another and our journey through life can be enriched.

> Mentors are guides. They lead us along the journey of our lives. We trust them because they have been there before.
>
> —Laurent A. Daloz

A Compassionate Presence

. . . .

Our favorite theologian and spiritual mentor, the late Henri Nouwen, wrote in his book *Compassion,* "Compassion means full immersion in the condition of being human."

The word *compassion* is derived from the Latin words *pati* and *cum,* meaning "to suffer with."

Nouwen writes,

> Compassion asks us to go where it hurts, to enter into places of pain, to share in brokenness, fear, confusion, and anguish. Compassion challenges us to cry out with those in misery, to mourn with those who are lonely, to weep with those in tears. Compassion requires us to be weak with the weak, vulnerable with the vulnerable, and powerless with powerless.

> … the word compassion could be read as com-patience. The word passion and patience both find their roots in the Latin word "pati," which means "suffering." The compassionate life could be described as a life patiently lived with others.

A life of compassionate presence.

Certainly no one exemplified that kind of presence and patience during our lifetime more than Mother Teresa of Calcutta. Her presence living among, and caring for, those who lived in the most-searing poverty is an example of "suffering with" at its most profound.

Several years ago, following her death, her private journals and letters, *Mother Teresa: Come Be My Light*, were published. Her writings revealed a stunning surprise about Mother Teresa. Her writings were not the tranquil meditations of a saint secure in her faith but rather were the tortured feelings of someone confronting a season of darkness that lasted for decades.

In her darkness, Mother Teresa doubted the very existence of God. She wrote, "In my soul I feel just that terrible pain of loss, of God not wanting me—of God not being God—of God not existing ... I find no words to express the depths of the darkness."

Yet in the midst of this dark season, Mother Teresa concluded that these painful sufferings could help her identify with the abandonment that people living in poverty faced every day and could help her enter in the "dark holes" of the lives of the people with whom she lived and worked.

There was a reason she was sometimes called the Saint of the Gutters. She often saw the most horrible things this world had to offer. Those things distressed her profoundly and sent her into the darkness. Yet Mother Teresa never stopped providing a compassionate presence with those who were diseased, impoverished, and dying. She never abandoned them despite her doubts and her own anguish. She entered into their lives with love and a patience that often defied understanding.

She exemplified the patience that Henri Nouwen defined: "Patience means to enter actively into the thick of life and to fully bear the suffering within and around us. Patience is the capacity to see, hear, touch, taste and smell as fully as possible the inner and outer events of our lives."

In our own small and humble way, we try to model a compassionate presence, com-patience, with those we encounter every day.

For several months we had been listening to a woman tell us her story. It was a difficult, multilayered story filled with loss, unrealized dreams, and life-threatening illness. One day, after listening to her describe in detail the maddening reality of enduring the pain associated with restless leg syndrome, Tom asked, "Don't you wonder sometimes why life has to be so hard? I asked the same question last night, in the middle of the night, when I couldn't sleep."

Here is Tom's account of that day:

I had decided that moment to do something that would go against the standard protocol of counseling. Michael and I both believe that to establish trust it is vital for the people who tell us their stories to know some part of our stories too. To show them that we are human just as they are—humans who are vulnerable, who sometimes hurt, who sometimes are afraid. So I opened up about the condition I deal with every day, my struggle with fibromyalgia, a struggle that has been getting increasingly worse. I was in such pain the night before that I was ready to put my hand through a wall.

As I shared my struggle, we could both see and feel her comfort level with us increase noticeably. Her body language changed. She appeared lighter, brighter. In the move from just her telling us her story, to us beginning to tell her our stories, the chains had fallen off. She was beginning to be set free.

She related to my story. She expressed incredible anger too about those nights when her pain was most intense. She expressed how grateful she was to know that she wasn't alone, that someone else might understand at least some of what she was going through.

Instantly, she opened up more deeply than she ever had before. In the conversation that followed she expressed her anger with God, how disappointed she was in God's seeming lack of concern. She'd been holding this in for years; she never had anyone with whom she could openly express those feelings. But that day she did, and it made all the difference.

She had believed that God promises to give goodness to us. "It's an honest request, isn't it, to have something good come into my life? Not a selfish one either?"

We could see the frustration on her face. Her clenched teeth and hands. Her posture, defiant. She was angry with God. And she was trying to feel us out to see how we would respond.

She wrote to us following that day and expressed how grateful she was that we could empathize with her pain and frustration.

The one thing we could assure her was that God was with her in the pain, that just being with us was a supreme act of love. We couldn't explain why she had to endure her pain, and we didn't pretend to know. We didn't try to fix her, because we can't. We tried hard not to offer her any clichés, because they just aren't helpful.

We simply met her in her pain. We listened to her express it and allowed her to share all the emotions she was feeling. Being able to listen to it didn't take her pain away. It didn't make the questions more easily answerable. It didn't take all her darkness away. But it did allow a beam of light to shine through, and that helped her make it through another hour of another day. We simply entered into the thick of her life and let her know that we cared enough to listen to her pain.

Owning Our Stories

I've come to believe that all my past failure and frustration
were actually laying the foundation for the understandings
that have created the new level of living I now enjoy.

—Tony Robbins

. . . .

Tom

When I was in high school, I took a shop class that, to be perfectly
honest, I really did not like. While I'm not an expert, I do have a
few carpentry skills and am adept at crafting things with my hands. But
the teacher was critical and intimidating, and his method of teaching
made me feel like a huge failure in the class. He created an environment in
which perfection was expected. There was no room for mistakes. He was
fearsome; I did my best to avoid him as much as I could. My heart sunk
and my stomach churned every time I saw him coming through the door
into the shop for class.

One particular Friday afternoon, I remember my anxiety increased as
the day progressed. Shop class began at approximately two thirty in the
afternoon, and it was my last class before the weekend. I couldn't focus on
any of my other classes after lunch. I checked the clock every five minutes,
dreading the moment when final period would begin.

At 2:30 p.m. I sat down at my lab station. At 2:35 my teacher approached me as he did nearly every other day of the week and asked, loudly, "What are you working on today?"

Like most high school students, I often lived in the moment and didn't know what I was doing from one moment to the next. I said I didn't know. Truth be told, I really *didn't* know what I was supposed to be working on or what to do next. The project was something I had never done before, and it required tools and concepts I had not learned. The teacher then went on a long rant in front of the whole class about how people don't succeed in life if they don't have a plan of action.

That one moment spoiled the rest of my weekend. I couldn't stop thinking about what he said and about the humiliating environment he created. It's a strong memory accompanied by strong feelings that remain with me nearly sixteen years later. Those memories still haunt me. The lesson I best learned in that class was that if I was not perfect, then I was no good at all.

And that's not a very good feeling to have.

I wish I could say that a high school shop class was the only forum in which I have been afraid to fail. But that just isn't true. A big part of my life's story has revolved around this debilitating issue.

Michael

I remember my own high school story. For me the humiliation came in gym class. I was the smallest boy in my entire class, from day one of first grade to graduation day twelve years later. For most of those years my size intimidated me athletically. My short stature, 5'2" at the time, was most evident when we played basketball. I dreaded basketball days.

"Men, line up against the wall. Klein and Schaffner, you're team captains. Choose up sides."

My stomach churned. My heart beat faster. I knew what was coming; it always played out the same way. The shortest kid in the class doesn't get chosen first for basketball. Almost every time, his name is called last.

The usual names were called, quickly. We all knew the order: Bair. Andrews. Schuman. Aarons. Good athletes in multiple varsity sports. Each of them. Some of the tallest guys in the class.

At the sound of their names, they ran out to their captain. After the first string was called, they started whispering—not so quietly—to their captains: "Take Deal. Get Weaver. Himes. Schreiber." Not Gingerich.

It wasn't just the team captains who didn't choose me. The rest of my classmates didn't want me either. It was severely diminishing. I felt increasingly smaller. Left out. Unwanted.

It would, of course, grow worse as the other guys' names were called and mine wasn't. The longer it went, as I stood there increasingly more alone up against that wall, the more I fidgeted. My face was flushed. Hot. Red. I couldn't look at anyone. My eyes darted along the floor, up at the lights, at my sneakers. Anywhere but the other guys.

Finally, after what seemed like an eternity, it was down to me and one other kid.

Please. Please pick me, I pleaded silently. *Don't make me be last again.*

"All right. Miller, you're with us."

"I guess we have you, Gingerich."

Keeping my eyes from meeting anyone else's, I ran out to my team, knowing I'd be right back against the wall again. They weren't going to play me. At least not until the teacher made them. In fact, I hoped they wouldn't play me. My confidence was sapped—not that I had any to begin with—and I hated basketball. I hated the way teams were chosen. I hated myself for being short.

When you're a fifteen-year-old boy who desperately wants to fit in, to be cool, and to be popular, it was misery feeling the way I did. When so much of a male's worth, at that age especially, is based on his athletic prowess, feeling as if I didn't have any prowess was severely humiliating.

That feeling also translated into many other areas of my life, which at times was also debilitating and certainly discouraging. It didn't matter what else I may have had some talent in; being chosen last at basketball served as commentary on my worthiness in every aspect of my young life. The message I received was "You aren't good. You don't really belong. We don't want you with us."

Left out. That's how I felt.

It wasn't until I discovered as a high school junior that I could actually run faster than just about every other boy in my class—and began to be recognized for that gift—that I began to feel as if I belonged. It was incredible how that newfound ability changed many of my high school fortunes.

But should my ability to run fast be the measure of my worth, my acceptance, or my inclusion? Should running fast or jumping high or hitting far or catching often or kicking a ball into a net be the sole measure of anyone's significance? No. It's so much more than that. But at that impressionable age, I wasn't able to understand that.

Even though I understand it differently today, decades later, those painful memories can still be triggered. To this day, feeling left out is my deepest wound.

How many of us live with similar fears, insecurities, and memories? How many of us struggle with feeling not good enough, not worthy enough? It is each of us. In some way or another, with some thing or another, every one of us feels lacking and imperfect and as if we are disappointing others or letting them down. Even more, we are disappointments to ourselves.

No one should have to struggle with those feelings. None of us is perfect, nor are any of us gifted in every single area of life. Instead of condemning our humanness—our differing abilities and our distinctiveness—we need to celebrate what makes each of us unique and valuable in our own special ways. The fact is, our humanness and our uniqueness can compel us to work more closely and cooperate more freely together. We need each other to share our own special gifts for the good of us all.

Author, public speaker, and scholar Brené Brown tells this true story of a man who confided in her. His story touched us. Sadly, we hear many stories like it:

> As a child this man had been a passionate artist. But he winced as he described knowing from an early age that he would be happy if he could spend his life painting and drawing. He said that one day he was in the kitchen with his dad and uncle. His uncle pointed to a collection of his art that was plastered on a refrigerator and said jokingly to his father, "What? You're raising a homosexual artist now?" After that, he said, his father, who had always been neutral about his art, forbade him from taking classes. Even his mother, who had always been so proud of his talent, agreed that it was "a little too girly." He told me that he had drawn a picture of his house the day before all of this happened, and to that day it was the last thing he had ever drawn. That night I wept for him and for all of us who never got to see his work. I think about him all the time and hope that he had reconnected with his art. I know it is a tremendous loss for him, and I am equally positive that the world is missing out.

When will we learn not to humiliate and degrade the abilities of one another, especially the abilities that we don't possess? When will we learn that none of us can do it all or have it all or know it all? When will we learn that we need the best of each other, that which is within each of us, to make our communities, our families, and our lives the strongest and healthiest they can be? When will we learn not to belittle each other?

When will we learn instead to affirm one another for the unique gifts we have? When will we learn to celebrate the distinctive person that each of us is? When will we learn to recognize and celebrate the best that exists in each of us: the gifts, the grace, the goodness?

"If you don't own your story …"

Those words were spoken to us during a small retreat we took together at a Benedictine Abbey. We shared our meals with one of the monks there, a learned and spirited man in his eighties, who was very interested in the work we do.

"It is needed so much. Bless you for what you are doing, what you are offering. People need to tell their stories. They need to own them. Understand them."

What he meant and what we talked about was this:

It is hard to grow when we don't know what we need in this life, if we don't know who we are. It is hard to know where we need to go when we don't know where we've come from. It is hard to be healthy when we haven't allowed whatever pain and brokenness is within us to be heard and released.

He understood it inherently. In his more than half a century of caring and listening and of shepherding others toward healing, this pastoral soul instinctively understood what we have made a covenant to do together.

He understood the importance of providing a safe, nonjudgmental atmosphere in which others can share, to unburden themselves. He understood that our cultural tendency to shame, to diminish each other, to condemn, and to vilify is not an answer to our problems. He understood that we have to give permission to each other to express ourselves.

He understood that the gifts we carry within us need to be shared freely and without fear. This must happen for all of us to find relief from whatever keeps us from being whole. He understood that people need to be met where they are and accepted for who they are. He understood that we all have a story to tell, a story that needs to be told for our own well-being.

He understood that nothing in our lives, nothing about our story, is ever wasted or irrelevant or unimportant. He understood that we are all inherently valuable and worthy of love and respect. He understood our work. He understood it because he's been doing the same work, in his own unique and special way, throughout his abundant career.

"If you don't own your story …"

If we don't own our stories—the wonder, the pain, the tears, the joy—then we can never be fully who we are meant to be.

LOL

Against the assault of laughter nothing can stand.

—Mark Twain

. . . .

Michael

I shared time with a friend who for the previous seven years had been living in a marriage that brought intense challenges and heartbreak. Kathy and I and some other friends spent the day with her at Hershey Park, which is within walking distance of our home.

Our friend asked to go to the park because she knew that she desperately needed to have some fun; she knew she needed to step back from the everyday toll that her fractured relationship was taking on her. We thought it was a good idea too. She needed a release and relief, a respite from her distress. She had never ridden a roller coaster that looped 360 degrees before, and she was nervous about getting on one. After our encouragement and reassurance that the coaster would be safe and worth riding despite her fear, she agreed to give it a try.

I sat next to her, and from the moment the coaster took off into the air, spinning us around, taking us upside down, twisting and turning through corkscrews at more than fifty miles per hour, she laughed—exuberantly and uncontrollably. She laughed through the entire ride. It was nervous laughter at first, but within seconds of the first plunging hill, her laughter turned to delight.

She couldn't stop. She couldn't help it. It was exactly the release from deep within her that she needed. For those few moments, it took her away from her longstanding distress. It lifted her to a place where, for the first time in years, she could feel something beyond her pain. That is the power of laughter, especially when it brings a total release.

Tom

I have a friend who has been living with chronic pain for many years. He underwent major spinal fusion surgery to help give him some comfort from his pain. He spent many days in bed following the surgery while his body recovered, but his emotional pain remained untouched. Over the past few years, his family has experienced loss, emotional and spiritual discomfort, and disappointment. He has been unable to work due to his physical ailments, and the bills have piled higher and higher. His house has been burdened with one liability after another, and his children have also faced hardships.

Their story is almost unbelievable because it is loaded with such heartache—and it continues.

One afternoon, Michael and I were eating in a local Chinese restaurant. A man wandered in from the cold. He looked worn out; he looked as if life had been getting the best of him on many different levels. After glancing at the man a second time, I realized that it was my dear friend. We asked him to join us for lunch.

We made small talk for a few minutes, and then I asked him about his health and his recent surgery and recovery. He has a wonderful sense of humor, so I made a joke about how I was certain that his wife of more than thirty years would appreciate it when he was back on his feet. I kidded him about her finally getting some peace at home again and about how she probably thinks he should just suck it up and stop complaining. Those jokes and a few others like them caused him to laugh uncontrollably. It reminded me of how much we all need to laugh when life is hard. It seemed that he hadn't laughed that way in a long time. It seemed that his soul was craving a good laugh, even just for a moment. It helped him to rise above his pain and sorrow.

In the years we have shared counseling people, especially those living with life-threatening illnesses such as cancer, laughter has been an essential part of our conversations with them. Many of the people we have listened to grew to understand how vital it was to be able to laugh at the absurdities, the indignities, and complexities of diseases that were trying to rob them of their spirit and life. So many of them found laughter to be an antidote that offered respite, even for just a few moments. But even for those few moments, laughter gave them strength, a will, and a sense of peace about doing what they needed to do to seek wholeness and healing again.

Laughter can lift our spirits when life is weighing heavy on our souls. We can never diminish the essential role that laughter plays in experiencing joy, in regaining hope, in overcoming disappointment, in providing strength to persevere, and in opening the door to find healing from our distress. Laughter truly is the best medicine. Our souls crave it because it helps transcend the everyday difficulties and realities of our lives.

Mark Twain was right ... "against the assault of laughter nothing can stand."

The Road Less Traveled

Two roads diverged in a wood, and I – I took the one less
traveled by. And that has made all the difference.

—Robert Frost

. . . .

We have friends who are part of a large extended family, and they
have operated a very profitable amusement park in a resort beach
town for more than fifty years. They have been very successful by the
world's economic standards. Generations of customers and employees have
been loyal to them. One of the reasons for their success is that they keep
their prices extremely low.

We spent part of a day with them at the park one summer afternoon.
What we witnessed was a family taking the road a little less traveled. It's
something they do every day.

When we arrived, the senior member of the family and head of the business
was doing exactly what he does every morning of the summer season—
methodically separating the previous day's trash from what could be
recycled. How many heads of very successful fifty-year businesses spend
time doing a task as dirty and humbling as that every day?

Moments later, several tractor trailer loads of game prizes arrived on site,
unexpectedly, and nearly all the family members were on deck emptying
the trucks on a terribly hot day. Inside the park office, the wife of the senior

member of the family, who was living with cancer, continued to do her part. She folded rags that were used by the employees to clean many of the rides from the previous night, another unassuming task. The "president" of the company, their son, was cleaning up a kiddie ride where a child had wet herself, a regular part of his responsibilities.

Everywhere we went in the park, every family member was working hard to maintain a standard of excellence—and doing so very quietly, humbly, and honorably. Everyone did his or her job with grace, with patience, with good humor, and always with politeness. No job was too mundane; no responsibility was beneath anyone. No member of the family expected any of their employees to perform a task that the family members wouldn't do as well. Each one pitched in wherever they were needed, without regard to position, status, or name. They all exhibited a refreshing, modest demeanor.

While we were talking with one of our friends, near the park's entrance, three women walked by. One of them stopped to ask, "How much do you charge per ride?"

"Each ride ticket costs thirty cents, and if you buy multiple tickets, the cost per ticket goes down."

She gasped, shook her head, and exclaimed, "That's incredible!"

Yes, it was. Incredible that this family amusement park could charge such low prices and yet very comfortably sustain itself and provide a good living for so many family members and their seasonal employees.

A newspaper reporter was coming later that afternoon to interview the family patriarch, one of countless interviews he has done over the years for various papers, magazines, radio, and television. He had to clean himself up from his trash and recycling duties. Their style of business is a marvel, one that is highlighted often in publications regionally and around the country. It is a unique family endeavor that has provided an abundance of profit and security to each family member.

Their success has been grounded in treating one another, their employees, and their customers with respect, with a generous spirit, and with love. This family has established its own philanthropic arm, donating to many individuals, charities, and missions that enrich the community and the world around them. They do not run their business with a sense of competitiveness and drivenness. Their uniforms—shorts and polo shirts—are worn by family members and other employees alike. Everyone dresses the same; no distinctions are made through their clothing. The only distinctions come in the attitude of service they exhibit, respectfully offering an atmosphere in which families can have memorable and affordable fun.

Their model and example humble us. Theirs is a way that we truly believe is better, a road less traveled that truly enhances this world and the common good. We are inspired as well to serve with that same attitude, and we believe that it is something the world sorely needs and that life is better for it. Our hope is that together we would follow their example and model and encourage others to follow it too—the road less traveled, because it is a route that makes all the difference.

Sacred Places

Your sacred space is where you can find yourself again and again.

—Joseph Campbell

. . . .

It is two nights before Christmas 2010. We are sitting in front of the huge stone fireplace in the Iberian Lounge at the Hotel Hershey, in Hershey, Pennsylvania. The room is beautiful, decorated for the season, dimly lit, warm, and inviting.

That night it becomes a sacred place for us.

We order something to drink and toast, "Merry Christmas!"

We sit back, soothed by the fire in front of us, grateful for this season. We are relaxed and comfortable. It is good to take this evening to celebrate Christmas together. We exchange gifts. We have no agenda except to enjoy a relaxing holiday evening together. We both feel very open tonight. Reflective. Willing to share.

It doesn't take long. We talk about friendship and find ourselves revealing times when friends have hurt us or let us down. We discuss what we need in a friend, how it is vital to us both to have more than superficial relationships. We both crave emotionally intimate relationships, in which

172

we can be mutually fully human, vulnerable, and unashamed. We have this with our wives; we have this with each other.

We realize this isn't the case for everyone. But we all need someone who isn't going to judge or condemn, who is strong enough to accept our idiosyncrasies and contradictions. Such relationships can be hard to find.

The conversation veers into the dreams we have for our futures—of places we want to travel and the legacies we want to leave. We also speak about getting married and having children at young ages. We share how grateful we are to have found partners in life who love us so unconditionally and patiently and who are inherently good for us. And we reveal regrets about things we've not done because we married so young.

We talk about some of our deepest fears and how we often feel as if we fall short. At times we can't wrap our minds around the fact that others have so much faith in us. And we admit that sometimes we still don't feel like real adults as our fathers are.

We share about what has left us feeling empty and unfulfilled in our careers. We speak about working with people who are difficult and who could easily rob the joy from our jobs. We have so many common dreams, common concerns, and common points of vulnerability.

Each time we take the risk of vulnerability by sharing things mostly hidden and personal, we feel increasingly safe with one another. An ever-deepening friendship continues to develop as we discover more and more about ourselves and each other. It is these moments that draw us increasingly closer together.

The Iberian Lounge in the Hotel Hershey is a sacred place for us. We return there every December 23, and every year we remember why it is so special. It's a haven of safety for us. It's the place where we were initially most vulnerable and emotionally intimate. It's the place where we realized that we were not alone, that we each had a brother who understood, who was willing to be fully human, who trusted enough to know and be known unashamedly, who wanted to love and be loved unconditionally.

Many of us have sacred places in our lives, places that by visiting them flood our emotions or hit vital nerves or tap into a reservoir buried deeply within. Maybe it's the place where a conversation changed the trajectory of your thinking. Maybe it's the place where you have gone when you just needed to talk through a dilemma, a place that always brings you clarity. Maybe it's a place that fills you with joyful memories of special people sharing special times. Sacred places are where the memories evoked are filled with utter goodness, absolute gratefulness, abiding security, and deep comfort.

We need to visit those sacred places whenever we can. Whether they are physical places or places where we go to in our minds, we all need to touch base with them, as often as we can.

To help heal our brokenness.

To remember who we are.

To know that we are not alone.

To know and be known.

To be fully human and unashamed of who we are.

Embracing Our Strengths and Struggles (Michael)

> When we're looking for compassion, we need someone who is deeply rooted, is able to bend and, most of all, embraces us for our strengths and struggles.
>
> —Brené Brown

. . . .

I was coleading a class for people undergoing trauma in their lives. One woman clearly needed to share her story, and it was a story filled with pain and fear. During a break in the class, she pulled me aside and started to tell me her story even though I had already heard most of it during the class discussions. A few minutes into her story, one of the class co-leaders walked by and heard what she was saying. He stopped, looked at us, and said to the woman, "You've already told me and several others this; you don't need to keep telling it. Don't waste his time."

I was stunned by his insensitivity. As he walked away and was out of earshot, I indicated to the woman that it was okay; she could share whatever she needed to share.

And it really was okay.

It was necessary for her, as she struggled with a life-threatening situation, to get it out, to talk about how she was feeling and how it affected her.

She felt lonely. She was scared. She was tired of it all. She simply needed someone to know how she was feeling. She needed to keep telling her story until she had processed it completely and didn't need to tell it anymore.

My coleader didn't understand that. He didn't have the patience or compassion to listen and to allow her to seek the emotional and spiritual healing she needed. Several times he chastised me for my "patience." He indicated that it was not a virtue. But even though he did not value my understanding of compassionate patience, I refused to be dissuaded from doing what I have always thought was right—to give others the time and the focus they need to help them find their way through dark and discouraging times.

Weakness (Tom)

(An Entry from My Journal)

. . . .

As you can see, it has been a long time since I journaled last, and much has happened. We have gotten more and more involved at church, which has brought many high and low moments for sure. I have started seeing things about myself that I have *never* noticed, especially some of the ugliness. At times, I have felt ugly, very ugly. Saturday night was one of those moments.

On Sunday I spoke at church, and leading up to the message, some of my ugliness came out.

On Saturday evening at around eight thirty, I've had enough. I've had computer troubles all day, I've worked all morning until two in the afternoon, I've had to watch our son Luke until three thirty, and I still have much prep work to do. I go to the local park (where I am now), and I start pacing, going over my message until I have a decent handle on it (although I still feel somewhat unprepared). When I get home, I go to print off the message, and the printer stops working. I drive—actually I stress and start verbally expressing my anger—to the local computer store to figure out the problem. They help me fix the problem, thankfully! I get home, start working on the PowerPoint until just about the time Sarah arrives home from work, which is eight o'clock. I quickly eat a meal and am about to start unwinding ... until Sarah tries to start the computer. It doesn't work, so she restarts it. She then tries to open my PowerPoint. It doesn't open. The stress builds. Now I try opening the document; still no luck. The stress level increases.

Now what do I do? Do I take a deep breath? Do I take a minute to "be still and trust God" with the situation?

Nope … I flip out. I start yelling. Actually, I first put my head in my hands saying, "What am I going to do now?"

Then I start yelling. I can't remember exactly what I said, but I know it was something like this: "I can't believe this; I can't believe this! What am I going to do? *I can't believe this!* I don't even want to do this tomorrow. *I hate this!*"

I look out the window, and my "Christian" neighbor is, or was, standing on my front steps. He isn't now. He turns and walks away. The tension rises even more. Did he hear me? He couldn't have heard me, could he have? I turn and look out the window. *The window!* Oh no, both windows are open—*wide open.*

I don't have time to think about this right now. I have to redo my PowerPoint, the PowerPoint I spent two hours on. It is now eight thirty. I am so tired and anxious I can't focus. I keep saying, "This sucks. This really sucks. I can't find anything."

Sarah grabs the computer and says, "Let me find what you need."

I grab the computer back and shout, "No! *No!* I'll get this done." I'm grinding my teeth.

About an hour later I am finally done, with the PowerPoint that is. I keep mulling over my message. I don't like the way this sounds. I need to take this out and leave that. I *need* to go to sleep. I lie down in bed; it is now ten.

Great. I can fall asleep now, wake up at five, having gotten seven hours of good sleep; that is more than enough, I think.

Ten fifteen, still awake. No problem—as long as I'm out by ten thirty, I'm fine. Ten forty-five, still awake. Now I'm getting angry. I flip my pillow over hoping the coolness of the pillow will help dry my head and neck and help ease some of the tension. Nope. It's eleven, and I can't fall asleep. I hop out of bed, throwing my pillows to the ground and waking up my wife who is already snoring.

"This sucks! This *really* sucks!"

I can't sleep. I fumble around to find my glasses, knocking a glass of water to the ground. I race downstairs to the couch, thinking the change of scenery may help.

Nope, still can't sleep. I'm sweating now. The sweat is literally pouring off my forehead and neck. Twelve thirty is the last time I look at the clock. My jaw hurts, and I have a spitting headache; must have been grinding like crazy again. I really need to get that checked out. It's still dark outside. Good, it can't be after five o'clock yet! This is good; I have a few hours to go over the message before I need to be at church.

I arrive at church early. In fact, I beat the sound guy who normally shows up before everyone else. This is good; I can get comfortable until other people start showing up to set up the place. Ten minutes later people start walking in. My quiet time is over. The noise level increases as chairs and tables are slid across the floor. I try to find a quiet place to pray and prepare my heart to speak. I can't do it. I can't calm down. My palms are sweating, my mouth is dry, and my stomach is churning.

The time seems to go by very quickly now; it's almost nine. One hour until the service begins. I place a phone call to my mentor, hoping to hear his voice to calm my nerves. He doesn't answer. I feel alone.

I sit in one of the rows, and a few people come and sit next to me. Why did you have to sit next to me? I am speaking today. Can't you leave me alone for a few minutes? One guy notices that I have the microphone in my pocket so he says, "Are you speaking today?"

"Yes."

As if the notes in my hands didn't give it away? He asks how I feel, and I quickly respond, "I'm fine."

He then asks, "Do you get nervous?"

I want to say "Nope," just so he'll leave me alone. But I don't. I open my mouth and say, "I always get anxious before I speak."

Why did I say that? No, he really isn't going to leave me alone. He goes on to share about his speaking experiences and how he has struggled with fear and anxiousness. He says something about God using us regardless of our insecurities. I wish I could say his words helped, but they didn't. I just wanted to hide.

Nine forty-five. The stopwatch appears on the big screen in front of the room. 14:58. 14:57. 14:56 … The time is approaching too fast. I feel sick, so I start walking toward the bathroom. Out of the corner of my eye I notice a familiar face; it is my neighbor … *my neighbor!* The same neighbor who may have overheard my moment of insanity the night before. He walks toward me, and I greet him. I tell him that I am happy to see him.

Eleven minutes left.

I stop for a minute in the bathroom and splash some water on my face. As if I am about to step out of the locker room before a playoff game, I look in the mirror.

"I look like crap. I look tired. I look nervous. Get it together."

I walk out of the bathroom (locker room).

The service begins. I can't sing. One song is over. Two more to go.

The singing ends, and it is time for announcements. After announcements there is a break, and then I'm up.

"God, please grant me the courage and the confidence. Please say what you need me to say today," I whisper under my breath.

Break time is over, and I begin my message. "This week my wife and I celebrate our five-year wedding anniversary. In those years, we have moved seven times, and most of those haven't been by our choosing. We had a neighbor with domestic violence issues, a landlord who would bang on the floor every time our kids made too much noise, and just last week we had a neighbor call the police at one thirty in the morning because our son was crying too loudly."

I pause. Oh man, I totally forgot my neighbor was here! I recover well and make a joke about the fact that one of my neighbors is here ... and hopefully he isn't the one who called the police.

My message seems to go quickly; it does go quickly. I look at my watch, and it has only been about twenty-two minutes. But when I timed the message beforehand, it was supposed to be thirty to thirty-five minutes. On to the question-and-answer time. I pause for a minute to try to catch my breath. Obviously I spoke quickly, but was it too quickly? Did people focus on me and not the points I was trying to make? Only time will tell. I ask a few questions just to get a feel for the audience. I tell them to take a few minutes to reflect on what I said and to search their hearts to see if there might be something they need to receive today. The room is silent, I mean, absolutely silent.

Are people being that reflective, or was my message too much to handle, or did it just suck altogether? I ask myself.

After another minute or two passes, someone finally speaks up. Thank you, God, that someone is either bold enough to speak or gracious enough to bail me out. The person shares about how he has recently felt like a stranger among his friends and how difficult it is not to conform when he is around them. I offer a smile and then respond. Another person shares, and then another.

Phew, that is a relief! Another person speaks up and shares about how important it is to be real with our neighbors and for them to see us even in our weakness. In that moment, I truly feel a nudge to share about my moment of weakness the night before. I share about how difficult it is for me to speak and how anxious I can become. I share about the anger and guilt I expressed and my fear of being caught in my moment of weakness. I share about how I would apologize to my neighbors if they were there this morning but how important it is that they saw me for who I really am—a human being.

After the service concludes, my neighbor approaches me and gives me a hug. He whispers in my ear, "Great job. Thanks for your honesty." He smiles and then whispers again, "I heard you last night, and I wanted you to know that I forgive you." He laughs out loud and returns to my ear. "And one more thing—I didn't call the cops."

I gather my belongings, and I look over toward the other end of the room. My friend and mentor, Michael, offers a huge smile and walks up to greet me. He says, "Great job, you did awesome!"

Michael has been a rock in my life. He is one of the few people in my life who I am willing to share anything and everything with. Together, we leave church and decide to go out to lunch. Michael, knowing how much of a challenge it is for me to speak up front, says, *"I'm really proud of you!"*

The next day I wake up, and I am totally exhausted. I walk around the house like a zombie. I can't speak. I can't interact with my kids. I can't even work up enough energy to make food. The day goes by like a blur. It is about nine thirty in the evening, and I start roaming the Internet.

Someone who was at church the previous day sends me a text. "So about your message yesterday: Dude, you spoke too quickly. It's like you somehow have to prove yourself so you just ramble off a whole bunch of stuff and expect people to remember it."

His words hurt. I feel as if I have just been punched in the gut. I close my laptop and go to bed.

When I get in bed, I read something that talks about having to remind ourselves—especially when others say things that hurt us—of our belovedness. Thankfully, I am so tired that my friend's words don't keep me up. I wake up the next day at seven. I am still trying to process my friend's comments from the night before. I still feel uptight about Sunday, and I can't seem to get it out of my head.

After breakfast I leave for my first meeting of the day. I'm actually meeting my neighbor who came to church on Sunday! He said he wanted to talk to me and get to know me better. We sit down for coffee, and we immediately start talking about how crazy it was that he showed up on the week I was speaking. He emphasizes once again that he thought I did a great job and how much he appreciated and respected my honesty and humility.

I can't believe how quickly our conversation moves. He starts talking about some of his hurts and the struggles he has faced in his life. He is much older than I am, and I have much to learn from his experiences. I listen closely. Personal struggles, struggles in his marriage, struggles with depression, and other major life crises. The list goes on and on. I soak it all in.

He then starts asking me deeper questions. "So why do you think you reacted the way you did on Saturday night? Where did that come from?"

I can't believe he would ask me that! I think about saying, "Seriously, you are going to ask me that during our first time together?" But I hold it in. Here goes, are you going to let him into your fears and struggles, or are you going to give a surface level answer like "I was tired; I had computer issues; my PowerPoint didn't work; etc."

I take the safe bet and choose the latter. I look at him, and he smiles. He knows I am not being honest. He knows there is something more, but he doesn't force it. I pause for another minute, and I think, *Why don't you let others in? What are you afraid of?*

After another moment passes, I straighten up, take a sip of coffee, then speak from my heart. "Honestly. Honestly, speaking in front of a large group of people is where I feel totally insecure;

I feel like I don't measure up. I feel like I'm never good enough and that I shouldn't be the one doing this because I don't have much to offer. So I get anxious every time I'm asked to do it, which sometimes leads to anger, fear, and resentment."

He takes a sip of coffee and speaks from his heart. "Tom, you are good enough because God says you are good enough. You have what it takes because *God … is … pleased … with … you!*"

He pauses in between each word for what seems like an eternity. He then goes on, "The Enemy is trying so hard to knock you down. He knows your pressure points and the areas where you are at your weakest, and he is going to focus on those areas because you are a threat if he doesn't."

I say, "I know that you are speaking truth, but I have such a difficult time internalizing it; I feel so numb half the time. I could hear those words over and over again, but they just don't seem to sink in."

We end our time together in prayer. He is obviously someone who has spent a lot of time in prayer and meditation. As we head toward our cars, I ask him, "Now that you know some of the struggles and where I am the weakest, would you be willing to pray for me regularly? Would you pray for these truths about myself to penetrate my heart?"

He quickly responds, "*I would be honored to!*"

We walk another few steps away, and he shouts in my direction, "Did you know that your other neighbors were there on Sunday too?"

"Are you serious?!"

God is incredible. There are many ways he will use us—even in our weakest moments—to have an impact for his kingdom if we will simply be obedient to his call.

***

For the bulk of my life, I wrestled with self-doubt and anxiety about whether or not I had something to offer to the world. Another example of this wrestling came when my first published essay, "Uncovered," hit the stores in *Chicken Soup for the Soul: The Power of Positive*. Michael encouraged me to share the story and its publication on Facebook. But because of my struggle with self-doubt and self-worth I was very reluctant to do it. I had to be convinced that it was okay, that it wasn't prideful, self-promoting, or arrogant. I needed to be convinced that what I had written and what had been published really was of value enough to be shared.

I thought, *Who am I to get something published? Who am I that anyone would care to read what I think? Who am I that anyone would care what I have to say? And pay money for it?*

I posted my story even though I still grappled with some self-doubt about sharing it. But that's why we all need encouragement and affirmation from others.

Self-doubt is a part of everyone's story. Maybe you are confident and successful in your career, but maybe you struggle with doubt about your effectiveness as a parent or partner. Maybe you worry that you cannot measure up in the business world, even though you know that your résumé measures up with the others around you. Maybe you are a writer and writing is hard, taking a lot of work and effort, and you have to be reminded that you have a gift for writing nonetheless. Maybe you feel as if you are simply not good enough in any way, to be loved or to be valued. In each of life's places of doubt we need to remember the gift that it is to have others in our lives who love us, who support us, who encourage us, and who build us up when we doubt our worthiness.

Both Michael and I were leading a group discussion one evening with people in their late thirties and early forties. But there was one man in the group who was probably fifteen or twenty years older than everyone else. During the discussion the older man said something very courageous: "I think that if people really knew the thoughts that went through my mind, they would be shocked and probably wouldn't like me."

We were impressed with that man's openness and vulnerability, with the risk he took to share something so personal, to reveal an inner monologue that wasn't always so nice.

The fact is all of us have thoughts running through our minds that we think, if others knew them, would cause us to be disliked, ostracized, or harshly judged. That man was speaking for all of us. But we have often seen that when someone in a discussion takes a risk and shares something very personal and potentially damaging to their reputation, something miraculous can occur. When one person shares, another person will often open up too, confessing to the very same feelings, thoughts, experiences, and reactions. So often when this happens, walls come down, and deeper friendships are born.

The key is to continue to have others in our lives with whom we can share this journey and know that we are loved and that we are safe.

Our hearts break when we think about those who have been shamed into denying who they are or feel forced to be constrained or restrained from telling their stories and from being their best selves. Controlled. Embarrassed. Inhibited. Guarded. Self-conscious. Shamed. All are words that keep people from being who they have been born to be.

None of us should have the light in our souls taken away.

The Most Terrible Poverty

Loneliness and the feeling of being unwanted is the most terrible poverty.

—Mother Teresa

. . . .

41° Fahrenheit.

New Year's Day.

She thought it would be cold enough to numb her body and lull her to sleep. Once asleep her lungs would fill with water, and she would drown. It would be peaceful, she hoped. She was ready to go. To escape the horror she was living.

The handcuffs she wore were to help ensure that she wouldn't try to swim, to fight for her life. She didn't want more life. She'd had enough.

The water in San Francisco Bay was doing its job. Hypothermia's effects were increasingly evident. Her core temperature dropped, and her blood pressure, heart, and respiration rates decreased. She was falling into a stupor, with growing mental confusion.

At a distance, she thought she saw something; it was orange and bobbing on the water's surface. It was getting closer to her, a loose buoy she thought. As it floated up to her she saw it had eyes, a nose, and a mouth. It was an older woman who swam daily in the Bay's waters, having trained herself over the years to endure its frigid, penetrating chill.

Oh, my dear. What are you doing out here? Are you swimming too?

She was angry and didn't want to answer. In her deteriorating mental state she couldn't answer. She didn't want anyone to know she was there. She didn't want to be saved from the water. She only wanted to be saved from this life, which meant dying in the water that day.

The swimmer saw the handcuffs, and she was now more concerned. She realized what was happening.

Oh, honey. What are you trying to do? I don't know what your troubles are. I don't know why you are trying to do this to yourself. But I know that Jesus can help you. If only you ask him, Jesus will help you.

Quickly, the swimmer raced toward the shore and notified the Golden Gate Park police. Even as the woman drifted further into lethargy, her anger mounted; she was angry that her plan was disrupted.

Within minutes an officer came toward her, riding a horse. The horse was swimming through the water. As they approached, the officer reached out with a hook attached to a long pole. Grabbing her handcuffs with the hook, he and his horse began pulling her toward the safety of the shore.

Blanket upon blanket was heaped upon her. There wasn't much hope that she would survive. But miraculously she began to thaw, both in body and in spirit.

Thirty-four years later we sat across the table from her and listened in rapt attention as she shared this unbelievable story. It was a turning point in her life, she said. We asked her why.

"When that old woman swam up to me out in the water, even though I was there to die, something inside me showed me that someone actually cared. I realized that God actually cared about me, that God would go to any length to get me back. Once I was pulled to shore, these words kept running through my mind:

> Where can I go from Your Spirit?
> Or where can I flee from Your presence?
> If I ascend into heaven, You are there;
> if I make my bed in hell, behold, You are there.
> If I take the wings of the morning,
> and dwell in the uttermost parts of the sea,
> even there Your hand shall lead me,
> and Your right hand shall hold me. (Psalm 139:7–10 NKJV)

"God was there with me. God came to me through that woman. I was given a new chance at life."

One of the main reasons she went into the water that day was because of the conflict she felt about her sexual identity. She had always felt different. She had always felt horrible about that difference because she was constantly condemned and criticized, especially in the church. Her faith was deeply important to her, and yet her faith tradition communicated the message that people like her were immoral, unworthy, and unwanted. Over time, hearing that message over and over again, it started eroding her soul to the point that she felt she would be better off dead than alive.

She felt the "most terrible poverty"—utterly alone and unwanted.

What good was it, she wondered, to be alive? What was the point?

As she told us her story, we could hear the complete and intense loneliness she had felt. A lifetime of hearing that she was no good stripped away any esteem she had and closeted her away in a prison of misery and hopelessness. She began to hate herself and descended into an abyss from which she believed she could never emerge. That self-hatred brought her to the point where the suicidal waters of San Francisco Bay seemed a better answer than continued life on earth. Death seemed like a sweet release from it all.

So she tried to end her pain in the Bay, to have her body swept out to the uttermost parts of the sea.

But even though she was living in misery, she came to see that there was a force pulling her back from the deep, back to life, back to find worth and her soul again. She was pulled back to believe, as the psalmist writes,

> For You formed my inward parts;
> You covered me in my mother's womb.
> I will praise You, for I am fearfully and wonderfully made;
> marvelous are Your works,
> and that my soul knows very well. (Psalm 139:13–14 NKJV)

In our time sharing with her, we wanted to remind her that she is loved, that she is significant, and that the world is a better place because she is in it. We wanted to remind her that the very tenets of her faith teach that love trumps everything else, that love always wins, that love is always infinitely stronger than hate and fear and condemnation. Our faith simply calls us to love and to let God shape us into whomever He wants us to be. For it was God who formed us from the beginning.

Conclusion:
The First Duty of Love

The first duty of love is to listen.

—Paul Tillich

. . . .

The fancy word for what we are called is counselors. But really, truly, we believe that mainly we are *listeners*. To be honest, there have been many meetings we've had with others in which we didn't have a whole lot of answers or much wisdom or counsel to offer. There have been times when we have left those meetings feeling as if we have contributed very little, not giving anything of much value. But so often, to our surprise, we will hear later from those people that we gave them just "what they needed," that we "helped them so much," that we offered the right encouragement and guidance.

And all we did was to listen.

But listening is really just what everyone needs. It is easy for all of us to come up with "easy" answers, sound bite wisdom or quick advice to fix a problem and find solutions, or to project our religious views or opinions. But more times than not, what people need and crave the most is someone who will simply be present with them. As Leo Buscaglia writes, "Too often we underestimate the power of a touch, a smile, a kind word, a listening ear, an honest compliment, or the smallest act of caring, all of which have the potential to turn a life around."

We both can recall the many instances in which we've been with people who are in grief, who have just lost someone they love. So often, we hear their friends come to visit and try to be supportive but end up doing more harm than good because they say too much. People have even asked many times, "What should I say to people who are going through a painful time?"

Our response is simple and consistent. It is far better to say little than to say too much. Essentially, all they need to say is "I'm sorry."

And all they need to do is be present. Just be there to walk with others through their darkness, through their pain. That is the most important and meaningful thing any of us can—and need—to do.

Tom

I remember receiving a phone call at four in the morning. The father of two teenagers in our youth group had died, suddenly. He was only in his early fifties. When I arrived at their house, his two teenage children greeted me at the door in devastation and tears. They invited me in, and for the next eight hours I simply sat with them, in their living room, listening to their memories, their stories, and their pain. I can't remember much of what I said. But I know that I didn't say much. I didn't need to. It would not have helped nor would they have remembered most of my words. They simply needed me to listen and to be present with them in their anguish and grief. That act of love—which is what listening is, that presence—is something they will never forget.

Michael

I spent months and months in the living room of a family that was broken apart. Anger, resentment, disapproval, and bitterness was crushing them all. They invited me in to listen to their brokenness, to help make some sense of their shattered selves, as years of pain came pouring out. It was raw. Some of it was hard to hear. But all of it needed to come out. I too don't remember saying much during those times, during those hours when their brokenness was starkly revealed. But I didn't need to. I just needed to listen. I just needed to be present as they told their stories. I just needed to be with them, accompanying them toward their journey where healing could be found.

"You saved our family" is the refrain I've heard often from the mother and wife. "You saved our family."

I take no credit for saving their family. I simply did what I knew to be right and simply listened. The healing came from within them, through God, through love.

That's what the act of listening can do. Through our presence, our gift of patient love—our gift of silence, really—shattered lives, families, and relationships can begin to be healed. The broken pieces can begin to be put back together again. It's not necessarily about "fixing" people, offering them advice, and telling them what we think they need to do. It's not necessarily about giving answers. It's first about establishing trust and showing one another that we can be counted on simply to hear and acknowledge what we are each going through. Then and only then can we begin to help each other find our way through the uncertain moments of our lives.

We encourage you to open yourself to be listened to and to listen to those who need to share. To be that quiet presence for those around you. To offer that gracious, generous gift of love.

> One of the most sincere forms of respect is actually listening to what another has to say.
>
> —Bryant H. McGill

We spoke to a group one afternoon about listening. We shared that we believe all of us have the need to be listened to, to have our voices heard and our experiences acknowledged. The people in the crowd nodded as we spoke. They understood that need.

We asked them if they had ever felt as if they were not always listened to. They nodded more vigorously. We asked if they could easily tell when someone wasn't listening. They indicated affirmatively that they could. We asked how it felt when they weren't listened to. Was it hurtful? Frustrating? Did it make them feel somewhat smaller? Diminished? Their eyes, their expressions, and the many yeses told their stories.

They knew what it felt like, and it didn't feel good.

To have others listen to us is one of our essential desires. It's one of our crucial, common human yearnings. But when we are not heard, when we feel unrecognized or unknown, we feel undervalued and unappreciated. Who among us enjoys feeling that way?

We cannot express enough how lonely and disconnected so many people are. Those are common feelings because so many people do not feel heard. But we also cannot express enough how significant it is when someone feels heard, how it lifts them and how it brings them value and a feeling of self-worth.

We spoke with a friend who has been struggling because he was finding no joy in his job. He has for many years been considering a career move, making a major change in what he does each day. At a meeting with colleagues one day he decided to take a risk. He spoke up, opening up about his struggle. He told his peers what he was considering. It was the first time he shared how he was wrestling with his future with anyone beyond his family or closest confidants.

And you know what he got for his vulnerability? No response. No reaction. A change of subject by the group. His admission was simply ignored. It was as if they never heard it. As if they never listened.

How do you think that made him feel? It didn't make him feel very good. He felt lonely. It definitely closed the door to opening up with that group again. It shut him down, and it inhibited him. Struggling to come to terms with a key aspect of his life, he quickly learned where he could not easily go for listening ears and support. In that moment with his colleagues, he felt diminished.

It taught him an uncomfortable lesson about vulnerability and about sharing his story. It's a lesson we've all, sometimes very painfully, learned. Not everyone will listen. Not everyone is able to take the story we tell and treat it with respect and value.

It requires vulnerability for us to be open with one another. Vulnerability is not always easy to show. But when we can find those who will honor our openness and our stories, we are very fortunate people indeed.

We hope that we can continually teach a different lesson. We hope that people can see and hear and feel the incredible value that listening can bring both to the teller and to the hearer. The lesson that includes the teaching of self-worth and compassion, a message about respect and love.

> Listening is a magnetic and strange thing, a creative force.
> The friends who listen to us are the ones we move toward.
> When we are listened to, it creates us, makes us unfold
> and expand.

> —Karl A. Menninger

But now thus says the Lord,
he who created you, O Jacob,
he who formed you, O Israel:
Do not fear, for I have redeemed you;
I have called you by name, you are mine.

Because you are precious in my sight,
and honoured, and I love you,
I give people in return for you,
nations in exchange for your life.

For the mountains may depart
and the hills be removed,
but my steadfast love shall not depart from you,
and my covenant of peace shall not be removed,
says the Lord, who has compassion on you.

– Isaiah 43:1, 4; 54:10 (NRSV)

About the Authors

Michael Gingerich and Tom Kaden are trained pastors, and they both feel a special calling to listen to peoples' stories. They believe that it is a sacred privilege to provide a safe place for others to share their experiences deeply and openly.

CPSIA information can be obtained at www.ICGtesting.com
Printed in the USA
BVOW05s1133240814

364025BV00001B/21/P

9 781490 839035